Manchester's first Modernist
KARL HAGEDORN
1889–1969

Manchester's first Modernist
KARL HAGEDORN
1889–1969

22 September – 26 November 1994
at the Whitworth Art Gallery, University of Manchester

25 January to 24 March 1995
at Chris Beetles Ltd, Ryder Street, St James's, London

ISBN 0-903261-31-6

Published by The Whitworth Art Gallery
University of Manchester
Oxford Road
Manchester M15 6ER

Acknowledgements

IN addition to those mentioned in my foreword, in mounting this exhibition, I have been greatly helped by my colleagues at the Whitworth Art Gallery who have kindly tolerated my giving it priority when so many other things called for attention. Among them, special mention should be made of Penny Hamilton, Sarah Hyde, Michael Simpson, Malcolm Todd, and Nicola Walker. Nichola Clark, a student of the University's History of Art Department, donated many hours to the process of helping me sift and list; to her I offer my sincere thanks. And I would like to record my gratitude to all the following who helped this exhibition to come into being: William Bradford, Helen Braham, Peter Burton, John Corr, Dr. Hilary Diaper, Jacquie Footer, Larry Keith, J.R.B. King, Sally Knell, Sandra Martin, Sheila McGregor, Max Nettleton, Helen Paton, Michael Pollard and Lady Isabel Throckmorton. Finally, I wish to mention the great commitment made to the exhibition by my secretary, Janet Nelson, and I wish to thank her, in particular, for her struggles with my ailing computer. I hope that all those who helped feel that their efforts have been justified in bringing this selection of Hagedorn's work to the public.

Designed by Max Nettleton FCSD

Typeset by Koinonia, Manchester

Printed in Great Britain
by Redwood Books, Trowbridge

Foreword

THE idea of mounting an exhibition of the work of Karl Hagedorn would have seemed rather eccentric, had it been proposed in the 1970s or 1980s. At that time, Hagedorn was known through his work that existed in public collections like the British Museum, Victoria and Albert Museum, the Manchester City Art Gallery and the Whitworth Art Gallery. It allowed him to be defined as an accomplished but conventional landscape watercolourist, who enjoyed recording what he saw on his travels, but who had played no real part in the continual innovation and originality which the twentieth century demands.

In 1990, however, the Whitworth acquired a painting by Hagedorn which revealed that, in 1913, his ambitions were towards breaking conventions rather than consolidating them, and which made it apparent that he was in sympathy with the most advanced art of the day. The acquisition of this painting (ill. 15) led us to Mrs Margaret ('Dodo') Harris, Hagedorn's niece through marriage, and her husband Richard. They kindly responded to our enquiries and, with their fellow Hagedorn Trustees, made known to us the story of the artist's early years. It is remarkable that Hagedorn's works of the teens and twenties had completely disappeared from public view, and the aim of this exhibition is to present it once again to the public, both in Manchester and London, where eighty years ago, it provoked violent reactions.

After almost a century of familiarity with what might be loosely described as 'modernism', visitors to the exhibition will find it easier to relate to Hagedorn's early 'cubistic' works than did the good folk of Manchester in 1913. Yet, they might still, understandably, have a greater respect for the more representational watercolours of the later period, or for the expert and invigorating design work. Thankfully, that is the choice which Hagedorn, and our century, offers us. In it we have seen the continual revision of artistic practice and of notions about art. I, for one, dread the time when art will cease to excite both belief and disbelief, when it will not both wound and heal.

Regretfully, I have been unable to uncover anything of significance about Hagedorn's textile designs, but this lacuna may offer students the opportunity for future research.

This exhibition has been formed by the generosity of the lenders, with the vast majority of the works and practical aid coming from the Hagedorn Trust. The Trustees were also generous with memories as well as memorabilia. It was a constant pleasure to be always hearing, from them, more about Karl Hagedorn, and to be welcomed into family homes and entrusted with familial confidences. I will always remember how much I enjoyed those 'research visits'.

Other lenders responded with great generosity. Some, naturally, wish to remain anonymous, but my debt to them is no less. However I am able to thank the Ivy Restaurant, the Coughton Galleries Ltd., Arthingworth, the Manchester City Art Galleries, the University of Leeds Art Collections, The Courtauld Institute Galleries, Mr and Mrs Martin Green, Mr L. J. Olivier and Mrs Susan Olivier and Mr J.G. Dean. To Chris Beetles, we are indebted for the opportunity to show the exhibition at his gallery in St. James's, London.

Finally, I would like to record my thanks to Richard Cork, Margaret Harris and Leslie Worth for their contribution of expert and enlivening texts.

Alistair Smith
The Director, Whitworth Art Gallery

KARL HAGEDORN | My Uncle James

Mrs Margaret 'Dodo' Harris

TWO of the charms of my Uncle James, as Karl Hagedorn was known to our family, were his eccentricities and his apparent inability to speak English other than with a German accent. Whether this was an affectation or not was never discovered, but certain verbal oddities remain clear in my mind. For example, the word 'booger' would echo around the house whenever he was frustrated, to the great delight of my young son Nicholas, who adopted it as the first word in his childhood language.

Another charming trait of Uncle James's was his inability to master matters electrical. For example, to remove a piece of burnt toast from a toaster, he would insert a knife with a metal handle between the elements without turning the machine off. The ensuing bang, small fire, burnt fingers and blown fuses would always surprise him.

Uncle James was a man of habit and certain rituals had to be performed at appropriate times. For example, a very old Christmas-tree fairy, which dated back to his own childhood, had to be woken from its annual sleep and placed at the top of the Christmas-tree, in spite of the fact that it resembled more a skeleton than a fairy, since it had climbed so many trees in its tinsel lifetime. We still have the fairy, and her bones are dusted down once a year so that she can dominate our own Christmas festivities.

For some six-and-a-half years we lived in Devon in a large old building called Membland Garden House, which had a market garden attached to it. This was paradise for our children and for Uncle James who would take his stool and wander from place to place amongst the woods, fields and hidden corners. The results of these expeditions were recorded in various sketch books but, alas, nothing spectacular remains. I think perhaps that he was too occupied with assisting the gardener in the building of bonfires, not only in Devon, but also at his own house, 7 The Little Boltons SW10 – a smart Kensington address. To his neighbours' horror he would light a bonfire from time to time at the bottom of the garden. Eventually a stiff letter from the Royal Borough of Kensington stopped this bonfire-building obsession. Other eccentricities of the Boltons, however, remained. For example, he converted the basement into his own domain with a kitchen, studio and bedroom – while his wife, my aunt Nelly Stiebel, was given the run of the ground floor which contained her own bedroom. I was not in the slightest bit surprised by the split, because the wine cellar for the house was located in the basement, and Uncle James made certain that it was restocked every week.

Uncle James's background is shrouded, to a certain degree, in mystery. It is known that his family came from Freiburg but the background of the family remains unknown, although some people have speculated that he was an illegitimate child of Kaiser Wilhelm II. To support this theory, they point to the fact that he looked just like the Kaiser, that he enjoyed considerable wealth, the source of which was kept a secret, and that his surname was Hagedorn, meaning 'Blackthorn', a name often given in Germany to illegitimate children of royal blood. However, it is known that he was presented to the Czar while on a family trip to Russia. A small plaque is all that remains of this incident.

Once when he and Aunt Nelly were on a visit to Malta, they were sitting on the hotel terrace when an English guest caught sight of Uncle James: 'My God. It's Kaiser Bill reincarnated.' Uncle James and Aunt Nelly packed their bags immediately.

He was brought up by two 'aunts' who did not lack private means. During his youth they spent many months travelling Europe, and he studied art in Paris for two years. He owned a property in Stockholm and a large house in Freiburg until he sold them shortly before his death. The 'aunts' were obviously a very significant part of his life and they died only shortly before his own death, both being well into their nineties. He visited them every year in Freiburg. This was a ritual journey and he only allowed his wife, my Aunt Nelly, to go with him once, on what turned out to be the last trip. He died shortly after his return to Britain while talking to me over the phone about his next expedition, this time to Venice with myself and my daughter Sarah Sue. He loved organising such trips, which were fun, but were inevitably chaotic. I called them 'Uncle's Travels on a Donkey'.

Uncle James's wife, my Aunt Nelly, was studying art at the Manchester School of Art when they met. Their only child Anne died tragically in 1928. This death affected Uncle James deeply and caused him to alter his style of painting. Uncle James requested Nelly to destroy all his existing work so that they would not be reminded of Anne. Fortunately Nelly ignored his wishes and hid the paintings in their house instead of destroying them. In later years she told her great-niece, my daughter, Sarah Sue, where the paintings were hidden. On Uncle James's death, the cache of works was uncovered.

My aunt compensated for the tragic death of their daughter by becoming one of the first lady visitors to a Boys Borstal, and she worked with young offenders for many years. She was obviously popular with the prisoners because from time to time she would meet 'her old boys' in the street and they would thank her for what she had done for them.

Uncle James was undoubtedly temperamental. He compensated for this by indulging in a large glass of red wine at about 10.30am daily. This would be followed by other glasses of wine as required. Occasionally he would indulge too much and close the day by performing a most wonderful Cossack dance. Unfortunately, the show was never recorded on film for posterity.

When it came to selling any of his pictures, Uncle James put up as many objections as possible to prevent the sales. He hated the process; his pictures were his children. Only careful persuasion and generous supplies of liquor would persuade him to part with a painting. He had a head for such negotiations, for they never rendered him drunk.

Finally, it is worth pointing out that he relaxed from the world of painting by disappearing off to the cinema of which he was a keen supporter. This support however, was limited to matinée performances when old age pensioners could buy tickets for practically nothing. He was content to watch the same film again and again if there was no alternative, and would make a point of taking my children with him. Sarah Sue will always associate *West Side Story* with Uncle James.

I (cat. I)
The artist, 1910, c. 1930

8

KARL HAGEDORN | A Memoir

Leslie Worth

I FIRST met Karl Hagedorn in the Spring of 1947, when as a young and rather nervous art teacher, I took up my first teaching post at Epsom School of Art. Karl was already on the staff, teaching part-time with a group of adult students.

I was impressed and a little in awe of this well-groomed, grey-haired gentleman, dressed in a very clean white linen smock and with neat bow-tie expertly tied, a skill I never succeeded in mastering.

Occasionally I met him coming from the station, walking briskly, his customary copy of the *Manchester Guardian* as it was called in those days, tucked under his arm. He would tell me of some of the exhibitions he had seen in the previous week: 'Have you seen the Minton drawings at the Redfern? I think you might be interested'. He had a broad knowledge, which he rather charmingly pronounced as '*know*-ledge'. An illuminating eccentricity, his mid-European accent became, if anything, more pronounced when he got excited. He was a regular gallery-goer and had a catholic taste - equally happy to discuss Jacopo Bellini or Jackson Pollock whom he stoutly defended if there was a disagreement in the staff room. But he was no sentimental liberal; gently radical politically, quick to dismiss ideas which he thought were humbug – his rather ascerbic asides were accurate and usually funny.

This cosmopolitan artist was in many ways 'plus anglais que les anglais' – he had a genuine affection for the Royal Family and knew all the relationships and could name their offspring – a Labour supporter with a shrewd appreciation of financial matters, not for nothing was he Hon. Treasurer of the Royal Society of British Artists, the finances of which he husbanded as effectively as his own.

Not long after I had joined the art school, he invited a colleague and myself to visit his home and to bring examples of our work to show him. This, I later understood, was typical of the interest and support he gave to the work of younger artists, as many who knew him would readily testify.

At that time he and Nelly lived in what I believe was a converted 18th-century coach house at Feltham, before they moved to Bolton Gardens. I remember it as a gracious brick building with high-ceilinged rooms and a paved courtyard, behind a tall brick wall. A fine della Robbia enamel, a trophy of one of their Italian holidays, hung on the wall near to the clematis. Inside, the rooms were tastefully furnished and he showed us his choice collection of English Staffordshire figures. He took us into his studio, which was elegant and orderly, quite unlike the picturesque disarray by which many painters, as I thought, evidenced their creativity. A large mahogany studio easel stood against one wall; there was a plan chest and a work-table and chairs; frames were neatly stacked to one side, pictures hung on the wall. Characteristically, he wanted to see our work before talking about his. His comments were complimentary and encouraging.

Eventually he did show and talk about his work, and his early days in Manchester when he worked as a fabric designer in the cotton industry, many of his creations being destined for the African market, a fact which amused him greatly. 'Just think' he smiled 'all those Nigerian ladies walking around wrapped in my designs'. He crossed over to the large 'double elephant' plan chest and pulled open one of the drawers.

Inside were examples of his early graphic work and illustrated material of various sorts – and some examples of his early so-called 'abstract' work. 'My wild "Fauvist" period' he said, apologetically.

He told us of his time spent in Paris, when he had studied, if that is the word, in the atelier of Maurice Denis. He had met Derain and once visited Matisse in his studio. He proudly showed us a cigarette which Matisse had given him. "I didn't smoke it, but slipped it into my pocket as a souvenir when he wasn't looking". The trophy was carefully preserved in a small tin.

When I first met him, and afterwards, he was largely known for his pen and watercolour landscapes. He was rather deferential about these and asked me what I thought of them. I remembered that I had mixed feelings about them. He favoured a stiffish paper, about a 200 lb 'rough' watercolour type, which I had thought a little unsympathetic. Incidentally, some of his paper was less conventional – he said that he always used pads of Izal toilet paper for printing his wood-engravings on – "It is absolutely marvellous".

He picked out one or two of his 'abstracts' . . . 'Perhaps it would have been better if I had stuck to these' he confessed. 'It's all Randolph Schwabe's fault – I showed him some of my drawings once and his comment was – "Karl you must learn to s-e-a-r-c-h" – It was the worst advice anyone has ever given me – destroyed me at a stroke! Ah well, it's too late now – let's have some tea.'

He loved to draw boats, and was very fond of coastal resorts in the South of France and in Portugal, particularly Collioure . . . 'It's spoilt now by all the tourists who go there; it was a quiet little place when Matisse was there.'

He knew that I came from the West country and asked if I could recommend some good places with boats – of course, there were many. I suggested Looe or Porthleven or Polperro. He was glad of the suggestions and came back triumphant one summer – sadly I had forgotten to mention the rain! Maldon in Essex was one of his favourite sketching sites but for this I could claim no credit.

Karl had a wide circle of friends and acquaintances stemming from his Manchester days onwards. He knew Neville Cardus when he was writing his incomparable cricketing reports for the *Manchester Guardian*, and as music critic too. 'I used to meet Cardus in Manchester sometimes – a remarkable chap – he had a rough upbringing – his mother was a prostitute you know.' (Was she? I never knew if this was true or not). Karl was well-read and spoke both French and German; I recall him helping me to compose a letter to a Parisian hotelier when my wife and I made our first visit to France together not long after we were married. He advised us to visit the Jeu de Paume and – ' you must go the Folies Bergères – I know it's mostly nude shows but the stage productions are quite marvellous.' We did, and nearly got caught up in a pro-communist battle with the gendarmerie at the same time – the show well lived up to Karl's recommendation.

He spoke enthusiastically of Bernard Berenson, but his 'bible', as he described it, was *The Science of Picture Making* by Sir Charles Holmes, one-time Director of the National Gallery. He lent me his copy once and advised me particularly to read the chapter on *Confusion of Symbol*. Compositional devices interested him and it was he who first explained to me the construction of the Golden Section in painting. 'I often draw up my sheet of paper in the Golden Section before I go out drawing' he said. Privately I did not think it made much difference – and in any case I would have found it too inhibiting.

A few years after we had first met, he advised me to apply for membership of the Royal Society of British Artists – the RBA. I did so and thanks to his support, I was elected (in fact both my wife and myself have been members for some time). In the early 'fifties the RBA was a very enterprising Society – artists like Carel Weight, Roger de Grey, John Minton and Kyffin Williams, to mention but a few, were recent members.

Finally, Karl gave up teaching at Epsom and our meetings, sadly, became less frequent. He continued to show interest and paid some visits to my Agnew's exhibitions – and bought a small watercolour of mine, of a frozen pond in winter with a lone skater (my wife) on it. It hung for many years on the wall of Karl and Nelly's sitting room in Bolton Gardens – and we have one of his, a drawing made in the Lakes – I think overlooking Grasmere and Rydal Water. My wife and I first met at this area when we were students, a fitting tribute from a spirited artist and a kind friend.

Leslie Worth is President of the Royal Watercolour Society.

KARL HAGEDORN

Alistair Smith

ON 23 October 1913, the second exhibition of Manchester's Society of Modern Painters opened to the public with an address by Frank Rutter, well-known as an art critic, and curator of Leeds City Art Gallery. Rutter, the North of England's most prominent supporter of the new art of the time, had recently mounted an exhibition of Post-Impressionism in Leeds under the auspices of the local Art Club. In his opening address in Manchester, he continued to champion the cause of experimental art, and was reported in full in the press next day:

> No one should dismiss the new art forms because he did not understand them. We were not born with an inherited instinct for the best in art, and our experience showed that it was the thing that we understood at first glance that soon became wearisome. The only artist who was sure of his place was the one who contributed some new idea and broke the little conventions of his day. Innovation was one of the qualities that made for lasting success, and because that was so the salvation of art might reasonably come from the amateur instead of the professional artist who had often to live by repeating himself to other people.
>
> Everyone was apt to get out of touch with the aims and ideals of a younger generation, and the stronger and more difficult they appeared, the more reason there was to study them. The two ideals that animated the exhibition were the expression of the joyousness of colour and the giving of an emotional synthesis to the artist's feelings.

Rutter clearly anticipated some negative reactions on behalf of the public. In fact, before giving his opening speech, he might well have already read some press comment since journalists had already had access to the exhibition. Their assessments varied from the basically serious, if guarded, to the rabble-rousing account in the *Daily Mail*:

> Manchester is moving. Not only is it to have tango teas, but an exhibition of all the latest phenomena in pictorial expression – cubism, post-impressionism, hyper-post-impressionism, futurism and every other '-ism' that a jaded art palate can be tickled with . . . Art lovers and lay critics are assured of a new experience . . . there are nearly 200 exhibits . . . a first hasty glance around the room is enough to reveal the uncommon nature of the pictures. Further study of individual paintings will please, puzzle, or exasperate, according to the taste of the spectator.
>
> Probably most controversy will be excited by Mr Karl Hagedorn's cubist pictures – 'rhythmical expressions in line and colour', as he calls them. Arcs and triangles of colour spread on the canvas with a free hand, they bear no resemblance to the visual appearance of any object; but as they are not intended to do so it is perhaps unfair to criticise Mr Hagedorn on that account. They will certainly 'keep people guessing'.

The correspondent chose to illustrate his article with a painting by Hagedorn (ill. 15) which he captioned as *A Washstand*, blithely contradicting himself since he obviously recognised the subject. In his article, *The Daily Mail* correspondent adopted a style of commentary which had already been employed by journalists and critics in regard to the Post-Impressionist exhibitions held in London in 1910 and 1912 when works by Manet and others were mercilessly lampooned in a manner which remains traditional within the tabloids to this day. The origins of this kind of scornful attack and of the disbelieving employment of specialist artistic terminology had originated in the distant past, but received fresh impetus in 1872, with the first unsympathetic reactions to what became known as Impressionism. From that time each new artistic movement has met with similar abuse.

Whether the article improved the circulation of *The Daily Mail*, we do not know, but the correspondent was determined to capitalise on the event. He managed to interview Frank Rutter on the day of the opening and clearly asked him his view of Mr Hagedorn's 'cubist puzzles', leaping delightedly on Rutter's reply which, a day later, he quoted under the headlines – Fauvism. Wild Beast art in Manchester:

> Mr Hagedorn shows cubistic tendencies in some of his oil paintings but in more of them, and especially in his watercolours, he shows great influence of what is known as Fauvism. Fauve is a French word meaning 'wild beast'.
> It was applied to those who had barbaric tendencies, and was accepted by them because it embodied their hatred of what was tame and conventional.

If the *Mail*'s primary objective was to promote controversy, that it achieved. It also served to alert the public to the event, which was claimed by Karl Hagedorn, who was Secretary of the Society of Modern Painters, and other exhibitors, as a resounding success. Replying to criticism, they pointed out that eight hundred people had visited the exhibition and that ten paintings had been sold. Indeed, this could be seen as a considerable success, given the fact that the exhibition was scheduled to run for just over two weeks and was displayed in what amounted to little more than a private house. The Society's members might have thought their greatest achievement, however, to be the reaction it elicited from Mr Frank L. Emanuel. At the Manchester Municipal School of Art he opened the annual exhibition of the Students' Union Sketching Club, by attacking what the *Mail* liked to call the '-isms' of art. In Manchester, he maintained, 'one realised the power and nobility of labour' . . . progress would be retarded by those who shirked work and joined an '-ism' group.

This type of reaction was surely what the Society had expected, indeed might have hoped, to provoke. Founded in 1912 by a group which included Adolphe Valette, it aimed to represent in Manchester some of the widely-spread tendencies in contemporary art. By implication, it sought to break what Rutter described as 'the little conventions of (the) day'.

Although Hagedorn was clearly the most advanced artist in the 1913 exhibition, he was not the only artist to be working in an idiom new to Manchester. E. Rowley-Smart, for example, painted in colours fiercer than had ever been seen in the region, and in a style which almost matched the extravagance of his demeanour. E. Carter Preston contributed some mysterious *Spirit Frescoes*. Other well-known figures exhibiting in 1913, were Bernard Meninsky and Valette himself. The Society included three members of the Sandon Club in Liverpool and, in 1913, four *invités* from Paris.

The artist who inspired most comment was, of course, Karl Hagedorn, and it may be that he delighted in the pitch of feeling he excited. Nevertheless, Emanuel's criticism struck home, perhaps because Hagedorn himself had been a student at the School of Art and perhaps because members of the Society were themselves active as teachers, some conducting classes in the very studio where the exhibition was shown. Valette, indeed, was drawing master at the Manchester School of Art where Emanuel gave the offending address. In any case, Hagedorn wrote to Rutter, asking him to publish a defence of the Society and its exhibition. Rutter declined:

> It is quite impossible for me to reply in the Press to Mr Frank L. Emanuel because personal relations between us are very strained. He has made many personal attacks on me with reference to the Allied Artists' Association in London. However, the Royal Manchester Institution has written me with regard to opening a public debate on 'Post Impressionism' so I hope I may have an early opportunity of replying in a more effective way.

Rutter did, however, try to arrange an introduction for Hagedorn to none other than Wyndham Lewis, soon to be the chief exponent of one of the new '-isms', Vorticism, and certainly one of the most determinedly avant-garde artists of the day. It may also have been at Rutter's suggestion that Hagedorn began

DAILY DISPATCH, TUESDAY, NOVEMBER 11, 1913.

CUBISTS DANCE TANGO IN FANCY DRESS.

2
The Closing Party of the Exhibition of 1913

3 (cat. **163**)
African Sculpture belonging to the Artist

4
Still-life with African Sculpture, 1915

to submit his work to the exhibitions of the Allied Artists' Association. These were conducted without a selection committee, all the works submitted being included in the exhibition, inevitably with variable results.

Within the Mancunian context Hagedorn's work was certainly the most advanced and this undoubtedly inspired a sympathetic reaction on Rutter's part. In fact, Hagedorn's work, and the controversy it created, was remembered, with something approaching pride, when the Society mounted its twenty-fifth anniversary exhibition at the Whitworth Art Gallery in 1937. At that time, William Grimond, a life-long friend of Hagedorn, remembered that the 'show (was) a very sensational affair dominated by Karl Hagedorn's *Rhythmical Expressions in line and colour* as he then called his large Cubistic paintings' (*The Manchester Guardian*, 6 May 1937).

Even more than eighty years after the exhibition, it is possible to identify precisely some of the works which Hagedorn exhibited, since his contributions were listed in the catalogue in three sections. Numbers 28 to 37 were all described as *Rhythmical Expressions in line and colour* (and priced at either eight or twelve guineas). These were probably the paintings described by Rutter as 'showing Cubistic tendencies', one of which was the so-called *Washstand* (ill. 15). Numbers 99 to 103 were catalogued in the *Watercolour* section and entitled *Rhythmical Expressions in colour and line*. They were priced at eight guineas.

Finally, Hagedorn exhibited four works under the heading *Etching*. Numbers 73a and 73b were *Rhythmical Expressions in line* (two guineas each), 81a was titled *Landscape* and 81b *Portrait* (each at one guinea).

In addition to the exhibition catalogue, two other forms of evidence aid identification. First, there is the photograph recording the fancy-dress party which celebrated the close of the exhibition, *Cubists Dance Tango in Fancy Dress* (ill. 2). The caption identifies, on the right, Mr Karl Hagedorn with Miss Elizabeth Orme Colles in whose studio the exhibition was mounted. Hagedorn is said to be in front of some of 'his own remarkable paintings'. In the corner, directly behind the couple, is the oil painting *Rhythmical Expression in line and colour: Fishing Boats* (ill. 23). To the right of the man wearing the skull cap and simulating the swaying motion of the tango is the *Ryhthmical Expression in line and colour* known as *Washstand*. Behind the head of his partner a larger work is seen to include in the top left-hand corner an image of one of Hagedorn's African sculptures (ill. 3), probably part of a *Still-life* (Hagedorn certainly featured it in a painting which is now lost but which is documented in a photograph ill. 4). It also appears on the poster for the Society's 1916 exhibition (cat. **49**).

From this it is apparent that the *Rhythmical Expressions* need not have been abstract, although this might seem to be implied by their titles — even in the so-called *Washstand*, for example, many objects are identifiable, such as the jug, bowl, bar of soap, shaving-brush, razor, bowl of flowers and windows. Naturally, we are more able to 'read' objects in cubist paintings (or, in this case, a cubist-derived painting) given almost a century of exposure to them, than were the good folk of Manchester in 1913. Another of the identified paintings also catalogued as a *Rhythmical Expression in line and colour* (ill. 23), is even easier to read, with figures, fishing-boats and their location all easily discernible. We can deduce either that *The Daily Mail* critic literally could not make out the objects or that he chose to ignore them, disingenuously, for the sake of sensationalism. The latter is more probable; yet it is important not to underestimate the perceptual difficulties which these new images delivered to the spectator. Even today, the over-riding impression is not of description, but of energetic linear pattern consolidated by the attack of vivid colour.

Some of the press comment was more responsible than that in *The Daily Mail* and this has the dual advantage of giving us a more accurate insight into reactions at the time, and allowing us to identify some more of the works which Hagedorn exhibited. A selection of the reviews are printed in pages 57–60, but the most significant passages are the following:

The cinematographic effects of Karl Hagedorn will provoke criticism for his 'rhythmical expression in line and colour' supported by over a dozen examples of cryptic sketches, may mean one thing at two yards distance, something else at four yards, or nothing at all at both distances. Naturalism and individuality may go together, revolt against convention may be expressed in temperate limits, as in the case of Monet or Conder or Lavery, but little gain seems possible from the bizarre or unintelligible.

(*The Manchester Courier*, 23 Oct, 1913)

To turn from Mr Hagedorn's vision of things, seen violently in prisms or recorded boldly in cubes, to the beauty and balance of Mr Preston's decorations, with their unerring sense of rhythm, their singing unity of tones and values, is to experience calm after stress, achieve harmony after experimental harshness. It matters not how one tries to make one's mood chime with Mr Hagedorn's, one is always haunted by the feeling that his works are so many experiments in pigments: that, let us say, allowing one to glimpse in flashes an ideal object through a kaleidoscopic jumble of tinted glass he becomes too preoccupied in refitting his glass pieces according to an up-to-date convention to care about the object.

(*The Liverpool Courier*, 23 Oct, 1913)

Mr Karl Hagedorn and Mr Malcolm Arbuthnot are the most modern of the moderns whose work assails the eye on these walls, and their visions, not to say nightmares, are a distinct shock at the first blush. Mr Hagedorn's rhythmical expressions include one which happens to be a sea-green man – Robespierre was pink to him – another seems like a kitchen dresser after an earthquake, a third a badly-broken stained-glass window repaired with coloured wools, and a fourth, of which the colour is undeniably harmonious and pleasing, vaguely suggests a rich tesselated pavement violently repressing any tendency to definite pattern. In the etchings the same spirit produces curves and cross-lines such as might haunt the Christmas dream of a schoolboy gloomily oppressed with thoughts of Euclid.

It is easy to poke fun at these grotesques, but if one candidly seeks their virtues there is to be admitted, in all of them, harmony of colour and a kind of mental excitement in the sinuous or angular antics of the lines – something of the kaleidoscopic dazzle, without the kaleidoscope's repetition of design. Sometimes the colour, especially in Mr Arbuthnot's work, strikes you as violent, barbaric. Perhaps he wants it to be like that, and he may take it as a compliment when we say it is just the thing to appeal to very young children. In fact these pioneers suggest Lewis Carrol in paint: as is 'Twas brillig and the slithy toves' to 'Sunset and evening star', so are these landscapes and buildings and amusing flicks and swirls of colour to 'naturalistic' painting.

(*The Manchester City News*, 25 Oct, 1913)

The *City News* critic, while adopting the usual negative, bantering tone, was able to propose that Hagedorn's work might have some positive qualities – 'harmony of colour and a kind of mental excitement' – and he was also able to grasp, and promote, the idea that Hagedorn's paintings chose not to be descriptive, that they sought to create something indefinite, and perhaps even sought to shock. In his assessment he may well have been influenced by Rutter's opening defence, given the day previous to publication, and, in particular, by his statement that 'we had progressed beyond the early Victorian idea that art was merely a question of representation. We asked of a picture not merely that it should tell us what the painter had seen, but what he had thought of what he had seen or felt. The painting must show the mental or emotional state of the artist'. Rutter was propounding one of the central tenets of the art of the twentieth century, which applies equally to literature, music, theatre and cinema, and Manchester was, for the first time, confronted with a new system of values in the visual arts.

From the three critiques quoted above, it is possible to identify, if tentatively, other works exhibited by Hagedorn and thereby to make our own assessment of his art at the time. 'Things seen violently in prisms or recorded boldly in cubes' might well have included catalogue numbers **24** to **27**, a series of female nudes principally in blue and yellow, one of which is dated 'Feb 22nd 1913', or even cat. **41**.

The 'sea-green man' mentioned in the *Manchester City News* is surely ill. 22, the painting now identified as *Portrait of a Woman* and dated 13. The journalist's confusion is easy to understand since the paintings in the exhibition were not labelled and the catalogue described the picture only as a *Rhythmical Expression in line and colour*.

The 'kitchen dresser after an earthquake' is clearly *Washstand* (ill. 15) while the 'badly-broken stained glass window . . . of which the colour is undeniably harmonious and pleasing, vaguely suggesting a tesselated pavement' could well be cat **42**, *Rhythmical Expression: Washstand?*

The etchings surely included items like cat. **9**, **10**, and **12**, which are certainly both geometric and atmospheric enough to have elicited the idea of 'a schoolboy gloomily oppressed with thoughts of Euclid'.

What is most remarkable is that Hagedorn was the only artist of the group to be working in a modern idiom. Since no other artist in Manchester had adopted an advanced style, this suggests that Hagedorn had been influenced by art which he had seen somewhere beyond the confines of the region. The fact that one of the newspapers described him as 'Mr Hagedorn of Paris' not only indicates a possible source of influence, but also suggests that Hagedorn was seen as a foreign presence, an impression doubtless consolidated by his Germanic name, his art and his accent (see the memoir by Mrs Margaret Harris, p. 7).

Paris did, indeed, effect a change in Hagedorn, as can be discerned by examining the work he did before he went there; but first it might be useful to summarise what is known of his origins and early training. His biography in the *Dictionary of British Artists working 1900–1950* of 1975, records details supplied by the artist himself, but which are amplified by Mrs Margaret Harris. Whether or not Hagedorn was descended from the German Royal Family, the other details of his origins are certainly known to be true. Born in Berlin in 1889, and brought up in Freiburg-im-Breisgau which lies almost directly between Strasbourg and Basle, he would have been about sixteen in 1905, when he came to Manchester to train in textile production. The notebook which he used to summarise his textile lessons shows his English improving through the years 1906 and 1907 when he was a student at the School of Technology. He also attended Manchester School of Art, and it was here that he formed friendships which were to prove to be significant, and where he met the fellow-student who was to become his wife, Nelly Stiebel. In 1908 Hagedorn, with another student, founded the beginnings of a *Freundschaftsbund* in the German style. Originally, only two artists were involved, Hagedorn and Francis Sladen Smith, and they entitled this miniature club *Der Künstler Zwei (Artists Two)*. Although the group expanded over the next couple of years, the name was to remain the same.

One of the activities enjoyed by this small art association was the creation of a periodical publication – a friendship book which was made by hand, rather than being printed, its distribution surely restricted to members of the group. The maximum number of 'copies' thereby created would have been nine, in 1913 when the membership peaked at that number. Among the papers left on Hagedorn's death was a bound volume recording the developing membership in the form of a growing tree. In the volume are drawings and watercolours done in the year 1912, when the periodical had reached Vol. 4.

The watercolours document, after a fashion, the travels which Hagedorn and Sladen Smith undertook together at this period. Scenes studied include 'Beni Mora', the region around Venice, Freiburg which Hagedorn would have wished to visit for personal reasons, and Paris. It was inevitable that two aspiring young artists would have wanted to spend as much time as possible in Paris for it was here, as has been said, that the artistic sun shone most strongly in the early years of the century. News, not only of Post-Impressionism, but of the development of Fauvism and Cubism, had reached England, much to the confusion of the Manchester Press. Central to this process were impressarios like Frank Rutter and Roger Fry, and the importance of the exhibitions which they organised in Leeds (in 1913) and in London (in 1910, 1912 and 1913) cannot be over-emphasised. These exhibitions brought to Britain the work of the continental avant-garde, with artists like Picasso and Matisse being seen on these shores for the first time.

Simultaneously, British artists were making their way to Paris and engaging on courses of study there, at flourishing schools which catered for scores of foreign artists. Most famous among these was, perhaps, the *Académie Matisse* attended by a large number of Scandinavians. Among the British artists who spent time in Paris and for whom that experience was crucial were Duncan Grant, Frederick Etchells and J.D. Fergusson.

Although we have no record of any connections between Hagedorn and the Scot Fergusson, the latter was to supply drawings for the periodical entitled *Manchester Playgoer* to which Hagedorn contributed an essay in July 1914. This certainly suggests that they knew each other, and warrants speculation in other areas. It is known, for example, that in 1911 Fergusson made a painting (now lost) entitled *Rhythm*, and this could easily have inspired Hagedorn's use of *Rhythmical Expression* as a title. Indeed Hagedorn exhibited a watercolour called *Rhythm in Blue* at the Walker Art Gallery's Autumn Exhibition in 1913. Further, Fergusson's association with leaders of the free dance movement of the time, like Isadora Duncan and Margaret Morris, may have helped to convince Hagedorn of the necessity of infusing his work with a pronounced rhythmic basis. The tango danced on the closing evening of the controversial Society of Modern Painters' Exhibition may be one more example of an interest in new movements and rhythms.

With Paris unchallenged as the centre of the world of modern art, it was only to be expected that Hagedorn and Sladen Smith would swell the burgeoning foreign community there. It seems that Hagedorn was absent from Manchester from early 1912 to mid 1913 and, given later references to the fact that he actually studied with Maurice Denis there, he may have spent most of his *Wanderjahr* there. Certainly, he exhibited work at Parisian exhibitions. One work in particular, (ill. 18), with a barge moored by a factory, excites speculation as to whether it was painted in Paris or Manchester. The answer may be that it was in Manchester that Hagedorn had developed this style of painting which sought to capture the distinctive poetry of the industrial townscape, substantially in emulation of Adolphe Valette, and had later discovered scenes in Paris which invited similar treatment. Thes watercolours of this time, quite freely handled, tend to have an overall, unifying tone generally of a rich blue, as do watercolours in the *Künstler Zwei* book.

The most significant event of Hagedorn's Parisian interlude was his meeting with Matisse. By the time the two Mancunians arrived in Paris, the French artist had closed his *Académie*, which would have held a natural attraction for them. After spending the first months of 1912 in Tangier, Matisse had now settled down to work in his Parisian studio at Issy-les-Moulineaux. It was there that Hagedorn gained admittance to him on the 24th of June, a fact documented in a way which symbolises Hagedorn's adulation of the artist. Until the end of his life, Hagedorn kept by him the remains of a cigarette which Matisse had offered him. He fashioned a little envelope for it and inscribed it twice:

Juni 24.1912   "24 JUNI 1912"
Besuch bei Matisse   CIGARETTE VON MATISSE
92 Rue de Clamart   IN SEINEM ATELIER mit ihm GERAUCHT.
mit Rik von Hool

Hagedorn, then, admired Matisse's work and would have been aware of the *Dance* and *Music* compositions which Matisse had undertaken for his Russian patron, Shchukin. The simplicity of the composition, with the energetic rhythmic figures outlined against a sparse landscape background, had a pronounced effect on Hagedorn, as several compositions of the period attest (cat. **16–22**). Matisse's adventurous use of colour contrast, in this period generally setting rose and bright green against blue, was also decisive, as were the melodious, rhythmic contours which he lent to both figures and objects. A photograph of Hagedorn, which must have been taken around this time, shows him seated in a boldly striped deckchair, with what must be one of his own works on the wall behind him – it is an act of homage to the kind of paintings which he would have seen in Matisse's studio on that fateful day. His *On the Beach* (ill. 20), which is dated 1912, is another example of the impression which Matisse made on him, yet Hagedorn has chosen to make the contours of both the clouds and the figures more regular and geometric than any that Matisse ever painted at that time.

Hagedorn seems to have returned to England in the early part of 1913 and the majority of the works which he exhibited in October that year must have been made in the ensuing months. Given his worship of Matisse and his *On the Beach*, it might have been expected that *Washstand*, *Fishing Boats*, and other works would have displayed the imprint of the French master more openly. True, *Washstand* employs the contrast of pink against blue so beloved of Matisse at this time, but it also indicates that Hagedorn had turned his attention in other directions. Indeed, it exemplifies the willingness of artists of the period to continue to experiment in various different ways. Hagedorn would have encountered several '-isms' in Paris, including Cubism and Fauvism. He reflects the former in his choice of still-life as his subject-matter, which was always a favourite with Picasso and Braque, the main proponents of Cubism in its analytic phase. Also indebted to Cubist examples is the way that the relationship between the objects and their environ-ment is re-interpreted by the artist, with the rear wall finding its way closer to the spectator, and the top of the washstand tilting upwards to offer itself to him or her, together with the objects laid on it. They, in turn, are described in a facetted way, rather like some of the nudes which Hagedorn had painter earlier in the year (ill. 5). The facets often include the shadows of the object, another way of correcting the balance between object and environment, as if the object is seen through the process of time which shadows log.

But other features of the composition show that Hagedorn had looked hard at something outside the various styles being practised in Paris. The sense of energy and movement in the exhibited works excited the word 'cinematographic' from one of the reviewers. This feeling of the repetition of imagery, thereby reconstructing the passage of time, which is perhaps discernible in the black-and-white works (ill. 12–14), shows them to be related to the Italian movement described as Futurism, which Hagedorn would have known in the emerging form of the Vorticist movement led by Percy Wyndham Lewis in England (see Richard Cork's essay). Finally, the small parallel barbs or vanes which run along several of the contours in *Washstand* were developed about the same time in paintings and designs made by the group who formed the Omega Workshops in London (cat. **149**, **152**).

Hagedorn, then, like many of his contemporaries, was searching for a contemporary mode of expression and employing the various new means which were at hand. The result conveys something of the energy which was universally felt to be part of the new century, and attempts to relocate the object within space and time.

How Hagedorn viewed his own works we know from an article which he published in the *Manchester Playgoer* of July 1914 – an article which shows him to have possessed the zeal of the reformer, if not the precise thought of the theoretician. He used as illustrations an etching of 1911 and a painting, made in the same style as *Fishing Boats*. It showed a view of Granville on the North Western coast of France, not far from St. Malo. Hagedorn's essay was entitled *Expressionism in Painting* and began thus: 'It was interesting work to introduce some time ago a form of painting, hitherto unknown to many people in Manchester' and continues: 'Original expression of individuality is the greatest form of art – only few have attained it and those few only by dint of much thinking.'

He then describes his development from the time when he was still fascinated by Impressionism (in 1910) to the time, three years later, when he learned 'to represent the intellectual as well as the emotional side that influences the pictorial subject, also to let these be the primary causes that prevail before the mere rendering of subject.' His final sentence becomes a rallying cry: '. . . . we should throw away old and conservative conventions in order to give encouragement and air to a movement that endeavours to create a representation and expression of our own period in its fullest sense.'

5 (cat. **30**)
Standing Nude, 1912/13

Hagedorn uses the term Expressionism to describe modernism in the widest sense. In the course of his essay he propounds the idea that art need no longer represent the subject in a conventional manner, since that function had been taken over by photography. Further, it is form which is the core of art:

> Arrangement must be and always will be the essential in painting, metre in poetry, time in music . . . . A day will come when people will see as much beauty in a decorative arrangement of lines and circles as they see now in a laboured masterpiece of the Pre-Raphaelite school, which may have taken years to paint.

And as examples of artists who have pushed the cause of art forward he cites Whistler, Picasso and Severini, the Futurist.

This, then, was Hagedorn's stated position at the beginning of the First World War when his most recent work had been recognised as having 'Cubist tendencies', perhaps the same tendencies exhibited to a certain degree, both by Britain's Vorticists and by the adherents of the Omega workshops.

The war, as for many, was to be an interruption for Hagedorn. For the first year or so, he was able to carry on working in a normal way and exhibited work both in Paris and in London. Being German, he clearly did not rush to volunteer; instead he became a naturalised Briton, and subsequently married Nelly Stiebel in 1915. As late as March 1916, he was still exhibiting at the Allied Artists' Association in London, where he received complimentary notices for his painting of *Bathers* (ill. 24):

> The best thing in this show that is so unequal – so revolutionary in one aspect and then again so mild and amateurish in another – is a singularly vivid impression, 'Bathers' by Karl Hagedorn (presumably a

Scandinavian). A company of young men entirely nude and of young women half-clad in sombre tight-fitting dresses are bathing from a tongue of grass-grown land in the midst of a lake overshadowed by bare green hills. The methods of the artist, if extreme, are in this case fully justified. The leaping, the diving, the swimming movements of these men and women, in the full energy of youth and strength, are given with surprising truth and daring.

(Sir Claude Phillips, *The Daily Telegraph*, 13 March 1916)

Another review identified Hagedorn and C.R.W. Nevinson as 'Futurists or Cubists or Synthetists, or whatever we may be allowed to call them'. (*Westminster Gazette*, 24 March 1916). And elsewhere:

Fortunately the Cubism of Mr Nevinson and Mr Karl Hagedorn does not sacrifice too much. By eliminating inessentials they intensify the reality of what is left; they seize on forms and colours, co-ordinating and harmonising them into a unity that becomes a true image of their feeling for nature without ceasing to be an image we may recognise.

(*The Westminster Gazette*, 27 March 1916)

Obviously, the critics had, to an extent, been educated by the artists. Certainly, May of that year when the Society of Modern Painters held its third exhibition in Manchester, a new critical awareness had taken hold:

We are very far from thinking that a painter has practised a fraud on the public unless he presents a recognisable and detalied likeness of a concrete scene. But if artists are to [produce] more or less abstract form, we are quite sure that oil paint and watercolour are not the best medium to use – the logical course . . . . is to turn to other materials – mosaic, stained-glass, embroidery, textiles or wood-inlay.

Mr Hagedorn's pictures, which are both more varied and more reasonable than formerly, need in this way to be presented in some material that would itself give satisfaction to the eye.

(*The Manchester Guardian*, 17 May 1916)

Despite the more tolerant stance of the critic, it might be suggested that Hagedorn had chosen to exhibit some less advanced work, for one item was entitled *Observatoire, Paris*, and may well have been done in Paris before he developed his modernist style.

A handful of works are traceable from Hagedorn's war years, and a few in the immediate post-war era. The opportunity to paint could not have presented itself too often and materials were scarce – the paper on which he drew one of his war-time companions (ill. 6) is of very poor quality. The few photographs which remain in the family's possession verify that other soldiers of non-British origin were part of his unit in the Middlesex Regiment where he rose to the rank of Lance-corporal.

As might have been expected he won first prize in an art competition while in the army for a work entitled *Labour Company Loading Trains at Bray-Dunes*. Bray-Dunes lies about 14 kilometres from Dunkirk and had been a resort before the war turned it into the site of an aerodrome designed to intercept German raiders on their way to and from England.

Other pictures allow us an insight into his war, for after it was over, he showed some 'battle-scarred landscapes' at the Allied Artists' Association in July 1919. These included *Dug-outs near Kundahar, Pelawar Farm near Wolverghem* (correctly Wulverghem) and *Devastated Area, Mount Kemmel* (possibly cat. **58**), all areas close to the front. Mount Kemmel itself was the scene of heavy fighting and alternating possession throughout Spring and Summer of 1918. Hagedorn was there in March 1919 to record the devastation of an area which was soon to be given over to cemeteries.

A month earlier he had created the autograph poster advertising a fund-raising event at Hazebrouck (cat. **59**), a railway junction which acted as a transport centre for the British army, after its liberation in August 1918.

Hagedorn's war works, and those made in the two years following the war are totally different from the earlier modern style. Their purpose is simply to record, as it were, camera-like, rather than to invent. After an obviously cheering trip to the Torquay area (cat. **60**), he settled, in 1920, to watercolours of the Northern industrial townscape, and of men at work, subjects which his erstwhile exhibiting colleague, C.R. Nevinson, had also employed (ill. 26, 46).

As Richard Cork's essay tells us, the force of modernism in England had been blunted by the war. The optimism and energy of invention to which the early years of the new century had given birth were replaced by a stunned conservatism. The coterie which had earlier committed itself to transform society through visual shock tactics now applied itself to an art which might console that public rather than energise it. It was within this climate, however, that Hagedorn created some of his most appealing work. He developed, in particular, two sides of his talent, each of which seems to be a logical development of his earlier 'cubistic tendencies'. Through 1922 and 1923, after moving to Derbyshire, he painted a series of local landscapes which fused the geometric principles of his earlier black-and-white works with his new concern for the recording of local landscape. In an amalgam of pen and ink and watercolour or gouache, he created some startlingly attractive and fresh visions of locations in Derbyshire and Cheshire (ill. 28–32). Looking carefully at these works, one becomes aware that these felicitous compositions, founded as they are on a harmonic, rhyming use of arcs and straight lines, constitute a positive, optimistic vision of the incursion of man into the landscape. This is no embittered revelation of the ills of the industrial revolution but a revival of Hagedorn's earlier optimistic belief in progress through invention. Neither did he attempt, at this stage, to disown his earlier work, as is borne out by the fact that he exhibited, in 1923, his *Still-Life with African Sculpture*, surely the painting of 1915 (ill. 4).

The foresight and planning which is evident in these watercolour views was clearly central to their success. Hagedorn made this clear when he gave a lecture to the Royal Society of British Artists in 1939. The core of his advice was towards the control of composition. He was most precise:

> You may have a half-Imperial sheet, say 15 x 22. In my reflection of the scene in front of me I have determined what I am going to get into my picture . . . having decided on my size I apply what is known as the Golden mean better known as the Section d'or. The proportions thus found by mathematics seems to be queerly instinctive in the human mind with a sense of beauty of proportion. The Golden mean seems to be an instinctive example of a fundamentally perfect proportion.

He then goes on to describe exactly how he carefully measured the displacement of intervals on his sheet of paper and how this process could be applied to making landscapes 'from your hotel bedroom at the sea-side'.

These habits, and skills, are as much those of the designer as of the artist, and indeed Hagedorn had, by this time, discovered in himself a talent for design. His early textile training must certainly have helped but he was willing to turn his hand in several directions. Most impressive, perhaps, are his posters and book covers (cat. **107–124, 141–147**) some of which achieved approval in the design press at the time. His *Buy British* poster of 1927 for the Empire Marketing Board (ill. 42) employs the repetitive, geometric forms reminiscent of Futurism, yet translates them into national red, white and blue. It is remarkable that television coverage of the Trooping of the Colour still concentrates on flattened overlapping planes and repetition of form throughout.

Hagedorn undertook much design work throughout the 1920s for charity. In particular, he designed the posters for

6 (cat. **52**)
Reclining Soldier, Reading, 1916/19

7 (cat. **87**)
St. Tropez (design for calendar), 1928

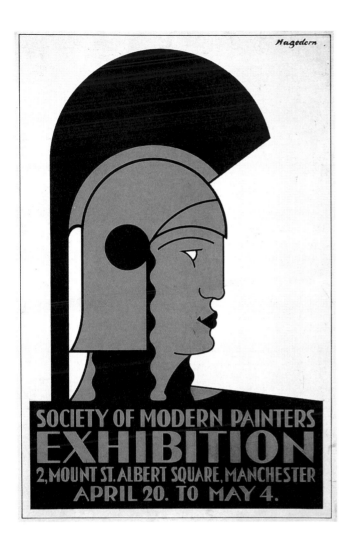

8 (cat. **108**)
Poster, 1926

9 (cat. **133**)
Cover of Radio Times, Summer 1929

the University of Manchester Rag Week, and his designs doubled as covers for the Rag publication, *The Rag Rag* (ill. 39, 40). Over a period of eight years, from 1924, he brilliantly reinterpreted the required motifs of sun and serpent in dazzlingly witty designs (cat. **141–147**). In addition, his Shippers' Tickets (cat. **134–136**) won him a Grand Prix in Paris.

A fair number of other design works exist, principally for textile firms, but also including covers and headings for the *Radio Times* (ill. 9), a publication which employed some of the best artists of the period. The *Radio Times* also published views of sites in London by Hagedorn. Most enchanting among the designs which he left, are a number of poster designs, which he obviously created as samples for potential employers (ill. 41). Each of them displays his rigorous sense of proportion, obviously the result of the use of ruler and compasses, and his bold sense of colour.

Just when, and why Hagedorn chose to revise his manner is somewhat in doubt. The largish landscape watercolours which he made while travelling (ill. 33–35), show a loosening of tension, and a gradual move towards closer representation. Three accounts of the change are printed here. Leslie Worth (pp. 9–10) tells that Hagedorn was convinced by Randolph Schwabe, a friend who bore high office at the Slade School of Art, that representation was the first duty of the artist – something which represented a complete turnabout from Hagedorn's beliefs of the teens. A second version, given by Mrs Margaret Harris, attributes the change in manner to the tragic death of his daughter at the age of twelve in 1928. She suggests that, in order to reduce painful memories, he disowned his early work which was consequently suppressed until after his death.

However, Richard Cork, a specialist in the period, points out that Hagedorn was only one among many artists who revised their modernist style in the aftermath of the war. A child of his time in the heady pre-war years, he was equally a child of the more staid twenties.

Whatever the truth of the matter, by the time he and his family moved to London in 1927 he was working in a substantially representational style, and the watercolours which he exhibited in the early thirties are in the style which he was to maintain for the rest of his life. He devoted the remaining thirty-odd years to his watercolour work, to teaching and to various administrative positions within the art community. Leslie Worth attests to his fascination with shipping, and several examples of his loving attention to the character of the small harbour are included in the exhibition.

Given the schisms which perennially exist within the art world between experiment and tradition, between abstraction and figuration, it is a delight to discover a career which encompasses all aspects. Whether Hagedorn's work is figurative or non-figurative, it always displays the firm geometrical base which he promoted in his 1939 lecture. And certain visual themes which preoccupied him in his pre-modernist period persisted to the end. His *Three Bridges from Cannon Street* (ill. 38) mirror his *Bridges on the Seine* (ill. 43) of about 1912. In each, he presents a poetic view of a receding townscape measured by overlapping bridges. Man's innovations in architecture and engineering occupy centre stage – surely a perception of the world bred in him by his training in Manchester, the city he adopted, and to which he brought modern art in 1913.

The British Avant-garde: from 'Art-Quake' to Armistice

Richard Cork

ON 5 November 1910, the art critic of *The Times* visited the press view of an exhibition as subversive as the Gunpowder Plot three centuries before. Unlike Guy Fawkes' thwarted Parliamentary explosion, though, this show really did blow up. Reeling from the combined discharge of the paintings assembled at the Grafton Galleries in London, the stunned and angry critic declared that the exhibition 'throws away all the long-developed skill which past artists had acquired and perpetuated.' Incandescent with fury, he concluded that 'it begins all over again – and stops where a child would stop.... it is the rejection of all that civilisation has done.'[1]

Today, the principal artists assembled in this survey are ranked among the most outstanding painters of their era. Roger Fry, the critic who selected them, wanted to concentrate on the great triumvirate of painters who dominated avant-garde art after Impressionism. Positioning Manet as their forerunner, he devoted most of the wall-space to an extensive range of canvasses by Cézanne, Van Gogh and, with the most generous number of works, Gauguin. Their impact amounted to 'the Art-Quake of 1910', as Fry's collaborator Desmond MacCarthy later described it, explaining that the show aimed at 'no gradual infiltration, but – bang! an assault along the whole academic front of art.'[2]

All the same, neither Fry nor MacCarthy could have foreseen the astonishing antagonism and notoriety aroused by their exhibition. During its three-month run, *Manet and the Post-Impressionists* quickly became the most scandalous art show ever mounted in Britain. It ultimately shaped the sensibilities of an entire generation, prompting Virginia Woolf to make the extravagant claim that 'on or about December 1910 human character changed.'[3] But few of the hundreds of visitors who streamed through the Grafton's rooms every day wanted to agree with her. As the exhibition secretary, MacCarthy had to supply a special book where they could write down their apoplectic comments, and the newspaper cartoonists were equally uninhibited. H.M. Bateman's drawing, headlined 'Post-Impressions of the Post-Impressionists',[4] showed a top-hatted gentleman arriving at the exhibition, dapper and dignified, only to totter out with buckled legs, gaping mouth and uncontrollable perspiration.

Why did the British public react as if they had been exposed to some appallingly infectious disease? Part of the answer lies in their ignorance of the art on display. Although the exhibits had mostly been produced a quarter of a century earlier, they seemed to the Grafton's shell-shocked visitors as alien and unexpected as the very latest eruptions in contemporary art. Manet, whose *A Bar at the Folies-Bergères* provided the survey with the first of its many masterpieces, was disturbing enough to eyes not yet at ease with Impressionsim. But Van Gogh's vehement distortions, Cézanne's brusquely-simplified forms and Gauguin's flat, pattern-like colours launched an unprecedented assault on the viewers. The cumulative effect of the 228 images on display amounted to a flagrant denial of everything they valued about art.

Some of the most virulent condemnations came from senior artists, who felt professionally threatened by the heretical Post-Impressionist innovations. John Singer Sargent, virtuoso concoctor of polished society portraits, opined of the exhibits that 'I am absolutely sceptical as to their having any claim whatever to being works of art.'[5] And Charles Ricketts, having resisted another critic's proto-Fascist suggestion that the pictures should all be burned, argued in favour of their preservation only because they might be useful to 'the doctors of the body and the students of the sickness of the soul.'[6] Once they heard about Van Gogh's mental torment, the most outspoken antagonists of the show did not hesitate to equate it with outright lunacy. Robert Ross, once an englightened ally of Oscar Wilde, announced that Van Gogh's work was nothing but the 'visualised ravings of an adult maniac.'[7] The normally liberal poet Wilfred Scawen Blunt was just as dismissive, deciding that the exhibition demonstrated the 'gross puerility which scrawls indecencies on the walls of a privy…They are works of idleness and impotent stupidity, a pornographic show.'[8]

In the light of such inflammatory comments, it seems surprising that the police did not descend on the Grafton, bolt its doors and arrest Fry at once. But the furore succeeded only in magnifying the show's scandalous attraction and sending even larger crowds surging through the gallery's portals. While astounded by what they found there, many visitors would have secretly savoured the illicit frisson of gazing at pictures which some even regarded as sinister symptoms of political unrest. The hysterical E. Wake Cook, writing in the *Pall Mall Gazette*, came to the paranoid conclusion that Post-Impressionism was 'the exact analogue' to the 'criminal Anarchism which accompanies Socialism like its shadow.'[9] What purported to be an art exhibition was nothing less than a dastardly smokescreen, veiling a threat to the very stability of the British Empire. And Fry found himself shunned as a pariah, even by many of those he had earlier counted among his friends. They could not square Fry in his new role with the man who, in the late nineteenth century, had become a widely respected historian and conoisseur of Renaissance art. A Quaker with a substantial private income, he had been Curator of Painting at the Metropolitan Museum of Art in New York since 1905. His reputation was so high that the Directorship of the National Gallery in London was offered to him – a post he declined. Known as a sensitive critic and a serious yet dogged painter, Fry became converted to the Modern Movement only when he saw two of Cézanne's pictures in a 1906 exhibition. Here, at the age of forty, he cast aside his former scepticism and began to convince himself that Cézanne, as well as being the true heir of the old masters, pointed the way forward. Fry agreed with the prominent German art critic Julius Meier-Graefe, whose widely influential book on *Modern Art* was published in English in 1908, that Van Gogh, Gauguin and Cézanne were 'expressionists' who inherited Manet's mantle and renewed his revolutionary initiative.

If the Grafton Galleries had not suddenly found a gap in their programme, however, Fry might never have mounted his revelatory show. It was put together in a hurry, and MacCarthy later confessed that he had 'never seen the work of any of the artists exhibited.'[10] Even Fry was still learning about the painters whose canvasses he now busied himself requesting from the Paris dealers. Looking back on the process of selection, he afterwards regretted his failure to acknowledge the true stature of Seurat, who was only represented by two pictures at the Grafton.[11] Acute pressure of time even meant that he let MacCarthy travel alone to choose the Van Goghs from the collection of the artist's sister-in-law in Amsterdam. Judging by the prices she was asking, extraordinary bargains were on offer at the exhibition: the best of Vincent's pictures cost £120 each, including one of the finest paintings from the *Sunflowers* series.

The crusading confidence which guided the show's selection was not accompanied by any certainty over its title. MacCarthy related how he, Fry and 'a young journalist who was to help with publicity' met to consider the show's name. Following Meier-Graefe's example, Fry 'first suggested various terms like "Expressionism", which aimed at distinguishing these artists from the Impressionists; but the journalist wouldn't have that or any other of his alternatives. At last Roger, losing patience, said: "Oh, let's just call them Post-Impressionists; at any rate, they came after the Impressionists."'[12]

In this rushed, almost offhand way, Fry coined the label which has henceforth been generally applied to the three painters dominating his show. But he demonstrated remarkable caution over the younger artists on view, the progeny whom the Post-Impressionists were supposed to have sired. Picasso and Matisse had only two or three paintings each, and Fry omitted the Cubist work which Picasso was then producing.[13] Its exclusion doubtless reflected Fry's own reservations about the increasingly austere and arcane development of Cubism. But contrary to his opponents' claims that he was merely iconoclastic, he may also have decided that Post-Impressionism was quite enough for the public to cope with in this particular exhibition.

Despite the vilification it aroused, *Manet and the Post-Impressionists* eventually came to be seen as a landmark event. Britain was at last forced to shed its insular ignorance and confront the radically-changing direction of European painting. 'There comes a point when the accumulation of an increasing skill in mere representation begins to destory the expressiveness of the design', argued Fry and MacCarthy's catalogue preface, explaining how the adventurous artist 'begins to try to unload, to simplify the drawing and painting by which natural objects are evoked, in order to recover the lost expressiveness and life.'[14] This, in essence, was the ambition uniting all the diverse artists in the show. And an emergent generation of painters in Britain was decisively impressed by the work they found at the Grafton Galleries. The old guard at the Royal Academy may have denounced it as 'nightmare art', but the most enterprising young painters realised that the so-called madness of Post-Impressionism had transformed the possibilities open to them as the new century asserted its right to challenge orthodox ideas. However urgently Professor Tonks pleaded with his students at the Slade School of Art to avoid the 'contamination' of the show,[15] they were enormously stimulated by its audacity. Nor was the burgeoning spirit of renewal confined to London. Fry's friend Clive Bell remembered how 'from all over the country came requests for reproductions, lectures and books about modern painting.'[16] The shock-waves sent out from the Grafton's seismic upheaval never subsided, and the disturbance it initiated soon transformed the work produced by the most adventurous members of a remarkably precocious Slade generation.

David Bomberg, Christopher Nevinson, William Roberts, Stanley Spencer and Edward Wadsworth were among the liveliest of the young painters influenced by the Post-Impressionist exhibition. Their excitement intensified in March 1912, when the Italian Futurists mounted their noisily-publicised and provocative London exhibition at the Sackville Galleries. Major canvasses by Boccioni, Carrà, Russolo and Severini[17] presented their disorientated viewers with a fiercely energetic vision, fired by the belief that the modern world was a blurred, whirling machine-age dynamo. Speed inspired the Futurists to rhapsodise about the industrial vigour of the new century, and the belligerence with which they announced their existence inspired some of the Slade students to adopt a new combative vitality of their own.

They were not alone in their awakening determination to overhaul British art. By this time, Fry had gathered around himself another group of painters committed to experimentation. Still an ambitious artist in his own right, he wanted to encourage the growth of mural decorations in the Post-Impressionist style. So he masterminded a cycle of large-scale wall-paintings in the dining-room of the Borough Polytechnic in South London.[18] Duncan Grant's *Bathing* was the most outstanding canvas produced for this scheme, and it proved that he had learned a great deal from Matisse in his search for rhythmic simplification of form. When Fry organised his *Second Post-Impressionist Exhibition* at the Grafton Galleries, in the summer of 1912, he included several young British painters in a special section. They proved that the spirit of innovation was no longer confined to the continent. Vanessa Bell and Frederick Etchells joined Grant among the Bloomsbury artists specially favoured by Fry, but the inclusion of Wyndham Lewis confirmed the fast-growing reputation of another painter bent on extreme renewal. 'The battle is won', claimed a triumphant Clive Bell in his catalogue essay. 'We all agree, now, that any form in which an artist can express himself is legitimate...We have ceased to ask, "What does this picture represent?" and ask instead, "What does it make us feel?" We expect a work of plastic art to have more in common with a piece of music than a coloured photograph'.[19]

Plenty of the visitors to this much-debated exhibition, which incorporated Russian artists as well as Picasso's Cubist work and Matisse's recent sculpture, still disagreed vehemently with Bell's argument. But a growing number of young British painters were sympathetic to Fry's standpoint, and some of them joined him in the founding of the Omega Workshops in 1913. There, working from elegant Fitzroy Square premises, they applied the principles of the new art to the decoration of walls, textiles, furnishings and rugs.[20] Commissions enabled them to produce entire interior schemes, most notoriously at the *Daily Mail*'s *Ideal Home Exhibition* in the Autumn. At this stage, however, Fry suddenly found himself under attack by a group of four disaffected Omega artists: Lewis, Wadsworth, Etchells and Cuthbert Hamilton. Accusing him of bolstering his own reputation at their expense, they stormed out of the Workshops and soon established a rival organisation called the Rebel Art Centre.[21]

Part of their initial plan was to compete with the Omega for interior decoration commissions. In the Summer of 1912, the most effervescent of all these schemes had been unveiled at the *Cave of the Golden Calf*, an uninhibited cabaret club run by the outrageous Madame Frida Strindberg, former wife of the Swedish playwright.[22] The underground premises off Regent Street were enlivened with clangorous murals by Spencer Gore and Charles Ginner, two leading members of the Camden Town Group. But Lewis's monumental painting *Kermesse* was even more startling, and along with sculpture by Jacob Epstein and Eric Gill it ensured that the Cave enjoyed immense acclaim. Lewis hoped to build on its success at the Rebel Art Centre. He carried out inventive schemes for settings as disparate as a Belgravia dining-room and a restaurant near Tottenham Court Road. But his formidable energies, as writer and artist alike, were mainly chanelled into the birth of an eruptive avant-garde movement: Vorticism.

Its advent was announced, in July 1914, by the publication of the aptly named *Blast* magzaine. Edited by Lewis, who wrote many of the polemical essays within, this high-spirited and belligerent organ set out to demolish the lingering legacy of nine-teenth-century culture. Despised people and institutions were blasted, others blessed. The principal thrust of the manifestos, however, centred on the emergence of a British movement to rival Cubism, Expressionism and Futurism. The Vorticists had no

11
Wyndham Lewis
The Crowd, 1914/15
Tate Gallery, London

time for the traditional still-life and figure-subjects favoured by the Cubists. Nor did Lewis and his allies approve of the rapturous romanticism with which the Futurists lauded the machine age. *Blast* placed the mechanised urban world at the heart of its concerns, but took a cooler view than the Italians. Britain, after all, had been the first country to experience an industrial revolution. Hardness, rigid definition and an utter lack of sentimentality were the Vorticists' preferences. Seeking to explain the meaning of the movement's name, Lewis told a friend to think 'of a whirlpool...At the heart of the whirlpool is a great silent place where all the energy is concentrated. And there, at the point of concentration, is the Vorticist.'[23]

The illustrations, scattered among *Blast*'s thick, typographically ballistic pages proved that a sizeable array of young artists were aligned with Lewis' cause. Apart from the painters who had stormed out of the Omega with him, the young London-based French sculptor Henri Gaudier-Brzeska, signed the manifesto. So did the precocious ex-Slade student William Roberts, and two women, Jessica Dismorr and Helen Saunders. Along with the poet Ezra Pound, who had christened the movement and promoted it in his critical writings, the Vorticists seemed set fair to make British art as vital and innovative as any of its continental counterparts.

Two outstanding artists, David Bomberg and Jacob Epstein, stopped short of becoming *Blast* signatories. But they shared many of the Vorticists' concerns. In July 1914, the same month that *Blast* appeared, Bomberg's first one-man show opened at the Chenil Gallery in Chelsea. It proved that, at the age of 23, he was already one of the most audacious and impressive painters of the British avant-garde. His most recent large canvas, *The Mud Bath*, arrived at a harsh, severely simplified and clean-cut way of defining energetic figures caught halfway between humanity and the machine world. 'I APPEAL to a *Sense of Form*', Bomberg wrote in his catalogue credo, explaining that 'where I use Naturalistic Form, *I have stripped it of all* irrelevant matter. I look upon *Nature*, while I live in a *steel city*. Where decoration happens, it is accidental. My object is the *construction of Pure Form*.'[24]

Jacob Epstein could easily have arrived at a similar statement when developing his *Rock Drill* sculpture. Commenced in 1913, it was his most experimental early work and celebrated, at first, the triumphant power of the white plaster driller straddling a black machine mounted on its tall tripod. The drill was real, purchased second-hand like a Duchampian ready-made. But the figure was modelled by Epstein, who displayed this towering ensemble at the London Group exhibition held at the Doré Galleries in June, and Epstein's stern assertion of mechanised, phallic strength would have appeared thoroughly at home alongside the work shown there by Lewis, Gaudier, Wadsworth, Roberts and their allies.

It was, however, the end of an avant-garde momentum rather than the beginning. By then, the First World War was already approaching its first anniversary. A growing number of avant-garde artists became embroiled in military service, and the opportunities for continuing to make work grew limited. After publishing a 'War Number' in July 1915, *Blast* was itself blasted by a conflict far greater and more bloody than anything which the Vorticists wanted to achieve in aesthetic terms. The sombre 'War Number' contained a black-bordered obituary notice, tersely reporting the death of Gaudier in battle. The urge to revolutionise British art, which had by now spread from London to excite painters like Karl Hagedorn in regional centres, would soon be obliterated by the accelerating horror of the carnage on the western front.

Nobody could have predicted just how devastating the war became. By 1916, when the Somme campaign caused even more savage decimation on both sides, the loss of human life had affected most families in Britain. Epstein summed up the gathering sense of trauma by making drastic alterations to his *Rock Drill*. After dispensing with machine and tripod alike, he lopped off some of the driller's limbs as well. Although the remaining figure was cast in bronze, he now looked wary and vulnerable. The embryonic form of a child, lodged so incongruously within his stomach, seems dangerously exposed. The forlorn, damaged driller peers out in search of possible assailants, unable to ensure the protection of the new generation about to be born.

There was a moment, near the war's end, when a surprising number of experimental artists were given the chance to work on monumental paintings. In Ottawa, the Canadian War Memorials Fund commissioned Bomberg, Ginner, Lewis, Roberts and Wadsworth to produce immense canvasses for a proposed building. And in London, a similar scheme for a Hall of Remembrance elicited remarkable contributions from, among others, Paul Nash and Stanley Spencer. Neither building was erected, and the paintings have spent much of their time since then in museum storage. They include some of the most powerful British art of the period, but the styles adopted in these images prove that the avant-garde had been forced to reconsider its pre-war priorities. The move away from abstraction towards a more representational idiom was dictated partly, at least, by the official bodies responsible for these commissions. Their demands, however, coincided with a widely-felt need among the artists themselves to retreat from the vision put forward in their pre-1914 work.

Before the war, they had regarded the machine as an agent of construction, placing its undoubted dynamism at the centre of their art. But the protracted devastation on the western front and elsewhere changed everyone's perceptions, irrevocably. In the first fully-industrialised conflict to involve the world's major nations, the machine emerged as an agent of unparalleled catastrophe. Never before had soldiers been decimated with such swift and callous efficiency. The wholesale annihilation caused by inventions as powerful as the rapid-fire machine-gun meant that all the pre-war fascination with urban modernity gave way to a desire for more tranquil alternatives.

Summing up his own change of vision, from an ardent faith in Futurism to a more traditionalist stance, Nevinson declared in 1919 that 'the effect of war has been to create among artists an extraordinary longing to get static again. Having been dynamic since 1912, they are now utterly tired of chaos. Having lived among scrap heaps, having seen miles of destruction day by day, month after month, year after year, they are longing for a complete change. We artists are sick of destruction in art'.[25] His comments help to explain why Lewis, in the same year, failed in his attempt to resuscitate Vorticism and publish a third issue of *Blast*. His friends' earlier thirst for extreme innovation was replaced by a need to re-examine their relationship with tradition. The experience of war had bred in them an overwhelming need for consolation. Nevinson, after a memorable visit to New York, eventually turned to landscape themes. So did Bomberg, who travelled to Palestine in the 1920s and underwent a profound metamorphosis in his approach to painting. Wadsworth, whose pre-war enthusiasm for industrial cities had been second to none, ended up concentrating on the stillness of seashore locations. Even the fiery Lewis spent an increasing amount of time painting portraits, and eventually realised that abstraction had been, for him, a cul-de-sac.

All over the country an urge to 'return to order' took hold. Even Paris, whose artists had proved so uncompromising in the pre-1914 era, became preoccupied for a while with the past. Picasso's neo-classical phase could hardly have seemed further removed from his earlier Cubism, and Matisse recoiled from the analytical austerity of his most rigorous wartime paintings. Hagedorn's adoption of a more conservative approach during the 1920s should therefore be seen as symptomatic of a far wider Europen phenomenon. The heady days of diehard rebellion were, for the time being, over. And when the avant-garde initiative revived in Britain, gradually gathering force through the following decade, most of its artists were too young to have visited the momentous exhibition with which Roger Fry had ambushed London on Guy Fawkes night over twenty years before.

1 Quoted by Virginia Woolf, *Roger Fry* (London,1940) p. 155.
2 Desmond MacCarthy, 'The Art-Quake of 1910', *The Listener*, 1 February 1945.
3 Virginia Woolf, 'Mr Bennett and Mrs Brown', from a talk given in May 1924 on 'Character in Modern Fiction'.
4 Bateman's cartoon was reproduced in the *Bystander*, 23 November 1910.
5 John Singer Sargent, quoted in *Art News* II, 16 January 1911.
6 Charles Ricketts to C.J. Holmes, quoted by Holmes in *Self and Partners (Mostly Self)* (London, 1936) p. 280.
7 Robert Ross, 'Post-Impressionists at the Grafton', *Morning Post*, 7 November 1910.
8 Wilfred Scawen Blunt, *My Diaries* II (London, 1920) p. 344.
9 E. Wake Cook, letter to the *Pall Mall Gazette*, 10 November 1910.
10 Desmond MacCarthy, op. cit.
11 See Roger Fry, 'Postscript' to *Vision and Design* (London, 1920).
12 Desmond MacCarthy, op. cit.
13 Fry preferred to include pre-Cubist Picassos, like the 1905 *Girl with a Basket of Flowers*.
14 Desmond MacCarthy, 'The Post-Impressionist', introduction to the catalogue of the *Manet and the Post-Impressionists* exhibition, Grafton Galleries (London, 1910).
15 Paul Nash, *Outline: An Autobiography and Other Writings* (London, 1949) p. 93.
16 Clive Bell, 'How England Met Modern Art', *Art News*, October 1950.
17 Oddly, Balla was omitted from the exhibition.
18 For a detailed account of the Borough Polytechnic

scheme, see Judith Collins, *The Omega Workshops* (London, 1983).

19 Clive Bell, 'The English Group', introduction in catalogue of the *Second Post-Impressionist Exhibition,* Grafton Galleries (London, 1912).

20 See footnote 18.

21 For a detailed account of the Omega rumpus and the Rebel Art Centre, see Richard Cork, *Vorticism and Abstract Art in the First Machine Age,* Vol. 1 (London, 1975).

22 *The Cave of the Golden Calf* is the subject of a chapter in Richard Cork, *Art Beyond the Gallery in Early 20th-Century England* (New Haven and London, 1985).

23 Douglas Goldring, *South Lodge* (London, 1943) p. 65.

24 David Bomberg, foreword to the catalogue of his one-man show at the Chenil Gallery, Chelsea.

25 Christopher Nevinson, interview with the *New York Times*, 25 May 1919.

Richard Cork is *The Times* art critic and author of the standard work *Vorticism and Abstract Art in the First Machine Age*, London 1976. His book *A Bitter Truth: Avant-Garde Art and the Great War* was published in 1994 by Yale University Press and a related exhibition is to be seen at the Barbican, London, from 28 September to 11 December.

12 (cat. **44**)
Rhythmical Expression:
Teapot, 1913/15

13 (cat. **45**)
Rhythmical Expression:
Landscape with Figures,
1913/15

14 (cat. **46**)
Rhythmical Expression:
Bathers, 1913/15

[facing page]
15 (cat. **37**)
Rhythmical Expression:
Washstand, 1913

[facing page]
16 (cat. **2**)
Self-portrait with Pipe, about
1915

Eric Newton
Caricature of Karl Hagedorn,
about 1920

18 (cat. **14**)
*Canal Boat moored by a
Factory, 1912*

19 (cat. **22**)
Walking Nude, 1912/13

20 (cat. **16**)
On the Beach, 1912

21 (cat. **28**)
Reclining Nude, 1913

[facing page]
22 (cat. **39**)
*Rhythmical Expression: Portrait
of a Woman, 1913*

23 (cat. **38**)
Rhythmical Expression: Fishing Boats, 1913

24 (cat. **47**)
Bathers, 1914/15

[facing page]
25 (cat. **48**)
Village Street, 1916

26 (cat. **64**)
Stockport, 1920

27 (cat. **67**)
Portrait of a Young Man
(detail), 1922

28 (cat. **72**)
Buxton from Westbourne,
1923

29 (cat. **71**)
Buxton, 1923

30 (cat. **73**)
Topley Pike, 1923

31 (cat. **74**)
Chesterfield, 1923

32 (cat. **70**)
Burford, 1923

33 (cat. **86**)
'Aunt Nelly in Avignon', 1926

34 (cat. **83**)
Col de Rodi, 1925

35 (cat. **84**)
*Continental Village with Church
and Tower, 1926*

36 (cat. **94**)
Beach Scene, Hastings, 1933

37 (cat. **95**)
The Large Tree at Kilton, 1933

38 (cat. **105**)
*Three Bridges from
Cannon Street, 1960*

39 (cat. **147**)
*Design for Manchester
University Rag Rag, 1930*

40 (cat. **146**)
Cover of the Rag Rag, 1934

41 (cat. **120**)
*Design for Poster: Washing
Powder*

42 (cat. **112**)
Poster: Buy British, 1927

Press Reactions to the Exhibition of the Society of Modern Painters, Manchester, October 1913

THE MANCHESTER COURIER,
Thursday 23 October 1913

ART IN MANCHESTER

The Society of Modern Painters

In Orme's Buildings, Parsonage, there will be opened today an Exhibition that continues in being until November 8th. The artists who contribute are members of the Society of Modern Painters. They are very modern, and it may be that some are very young. The motto they act on is that of Robert Louis Stevenson's mother in regard to her son:

Speak well o' my love!

Speak ill o' my love!

But ae be speaking o' my love!

You may be diverted or shocked. It is all one to them. One possibility is overlooked by them, however – you may be bored! For the work is far less individual than one would expect. The cinematographic effects of Karl Hagedorn will provoke criticism, for his 'rhythmical expression in line and colour,' supported by over a dozen examples of cryptic sketches, may mean one thing at two yards distance, something else at four yards, or nothing at all at both distances. Naturalism and individuality may go together, revolt against convention may be expressed in temperate limits, as in the case of Monet or Conder or Lavery, but little gain seems possible from the bizarre or unintelligible.

The effect of the Impressionists is clearly seen in the amazingly clever sketches of E. Rowley-Smart, who has much of Aubrey Beardsley's power to make detail fascinating. This gift is also seen in his striking portrait, 'The Misses Muriel and Gwen Pratt.' Occasionally, as in 'Storm Clouds,' he has strange success in other directions. In the examples of E. Carter Preston the first feeling is surprise at the anatomy of the models. Far better than the 'Spirit Frescoes,' though here 'The North Stack' is attractive, are 'Tewat Moss,' strong yet subtle, and 'Grange-over-Sands,' with soft grace and clever water reflections. Two of the best pictures are 'La lecture du petit lever,' by F.M. Buzon, and 'Vieille Femme de Fouesnaut,' by R.E. Plantey, though there is nothing particularly 'modern' in their style. Individual pictures of note are the 'Eskdale' of Elizabeth Orme Colles, and

a solemn 'Pennant End'; the delicate 'Madryn' of Mrs Ethel Martin-Frimston, whose 'Cartmel' has also good atmosphere; the clever 'Trafford Bridge,' 'The Irwell,' and 'Whitworth Institute' of AdolphValette; flower sketches by Mrs Kate Sargint; the strong but crude and geometrical sketches by Malcolm Arbuthnot; the 'Ramsey Promenade' of M.S. Nicholls; and the 'Vieille Maison' of F. Marcus Buzon, with clever effect. The most restful and not the least satisfying sketches are those of Mrs Kate Sargint, whose 'Homestead,' rich in colour, and 'The End of Summer,' with its waning sunlight, are both convincing. Of the sculpture by Herbert Smith the 'Fragment' and the 'Cupid' are excellent.

There is obviously no underlying tendency grouping the artists together, save perhaps a sense of decorative design, and despite the variety it will be found that the work, which is the least daring, is the most artistic.

THE MANCHESTER EVENING CHRONICLE,
Thursday 23 October 1913

PICTURE EXHIBITION

Impressionism, Post-Impressionism and 'Cubism'

The Society of Modern Painters has organised an interesting exhibition at Orme's Buildings, the Parsonage, Manchester. It was opened today with examples of the modern school of painting, works of disciples of Impressionism, Post-impressionism, and even 'Cubism.'

A small group of Manchester painters have organised the exhibition, and it is pleasing to find Liverpool artists, as well as Continental painters contributing. Impressionism is best represented by the pictures of Mr Adolph Valette, of the Manchester School of Art, his pictures 'The Irwell' (52), 'Dover Street' (53), and 'Swinton Bridge' (5), being worthy of special mention. In addition to the French lightness of touch and elegance they possess a quiet strength all their own.

With regard to the Post-impressionists, Mr E. Rowley-Smart, of Manchester, has some admirable figure designs in addition to watercolour landscapes and an oil portrait. Mr Malcolm Arbuthnot, of Liverpool, manifests a healthy, bold post-impressionism.

The representative of 'Cubism' is Mr Karl Hagedorn, of Paris, and his works are interesting, displaying abstract expression.

The exhibition is a highly instructive one, and should be well-patronised.

THE LIVERPOOL COURIER,
Thursday 23 October 1913

MODERN PAINTERS

The Exhibition at Manchester

Today Mr Frank Rutter, the curator of Leeds Gallery, is to open at Orme's Buildings, Manchester, the second annual exhibition of the 'Society of Modern Painters'. No doubt of pictures so intrepidly modern in spirit as most of these some hard words will be said; what will scarcely be denied, however, is that the society is richly justified of its title. Not that they conform to any single aim or type, these modern paintings; on the contrary, they cover a whole extended range of feeling from the clangours of Mr Hagedorn's 'cubisms' to the reticence of Mr Valette's nocturnes; from the diapason pitch of Mr Rowley-Smart's consummate portrait of 'The Misses Pratt' to the subtle nuances of E.C. Preston's 'Magical Morn.'

To turn, indeed, from Mr Hagedorn's vision of things, seen violently in prisms or recorded boldly in cubes, to the beauty and balance of Mr Preston's decorations, with their unerring sense of rhythm, their singing unity of tones and values, is to experience calm after stress, achieve harmony after experimental harshness.

It matters not how one tries to make one's mood chime with Mr Hagedorn's, one is always haunted by the feeling that his works are so many experiments in pigments; that, let us say, allowing one to glimpse in flashes an ideal object through a kaleidoscopic jumble of tinted glass, he becomes too preoccupied in refitting his glass pieces according to an up-to-date convention to care about the object. Not so with Mr Preston. He has given us a fine thing two or three times over, as the Greeks would say.

Excellent as Mr Rowley-Smart's landscapes, he is pre-eminently a decorative artist. Peccable in draughtsmanship, he designs with an incomparable grace. In his 'Salome,' rich as a Limoges enamel, and his watercolour schemes for episodes in Lord Dimsany's play 'King Argimenes,' one gets a hint of the Russian Bakst. Still, transcending these is that memorable oil study 'The Misses Pratt' and the 'Mrs Frank Forbes-Robertson.'

Of the two oil portraits of Mr Meninski one can only write that in poise and execution they are masterly; that is all. The tremendous verve of his five pencil drawings proves him to be conspicuously the most virile draughtsman in the room. Mr Arbuthnot has not convinced us that his daring has quite succeeded, while Mrs K. Sargent's landscapes please us fairly well. In sculpture Mr Herbert Smith has accomplished some engaging work, and we do not forget his 'Lemon Seller' or the simple dignity of his tiny bronze statuette.

THE DAILY MAIL,
Friday 24 October 1913

FAUVISM

'Wild Beast' Art in Manchester

Manchester will no doubt be disappointed to learn that Cubism has no place in the modern art exhibition which was opened yesterday at Orme's buildings, the Parsonage, by Mr Frank Rutter, curator of the Leeds Art Gallery. They should, however, be more than compensated for the loss by the knowledge that it has only ceded its place to Fauvism, which is, if anything, a more advanced section of the modern school of art.

Interviewed by a representative of The Daily Mail after the opening of the exhibition, Mr Rutter said: 'Cubism owes its growth to the desire, in the first place, to give the bright joyousness of colour to be found in nature, and secondly, to portray the emotional synthesis of the artist's feelings.

I don't see any Cubism in this exhibition. Mr Hagedorn shows Cubistic tendencies in some of his oil paintings, but in more of them, and especially in his watercolours, he shows great influence of what is known as Fauvism. Fauve is a French word meaning wild beast. It was applied to those who had barbaric tendencies, and was accepted by them because it embodied their hatred of what was tame and conventional.

Generally speaking, it is an extreme emotional reaction against the too intellectual and literal school of art. It is a crude, vigorous, and summary statement in which the main facts and the main emotions are stated without elaboration of detail.'

In his opening address Mr Rutter said: 'One of the great charms of this exhibition is that there is very little clever work. The work is sincere and expresses the emotions of the artist. Cleverness is a ban on art; it becomes a repetition and re-echoing of other people's work. Here personal experiments have been made by each artist.

Leaders in a new school have always been tardily received, and it is generally left to posterity to determine their real greatness. I ask of you not to label men of the younger generation as humbugs because you cannot understand or appreciate their ideals.'

THE DAILY NEWS AND LEADER,
Friday 24 October 1913

NEW IDEAS IN ART

Innovation the Quality that makes for success

Mr Frank Rutter, the curator of the Leeds Art Gallery, in opening the exhibition of the work of the Society of Modern Painters, in Manchester, yesterday spoke of the place and treatment of new ideas in art. The more there was in a picture, he said, the longer it took to understand it, and the greatest difficulty of all was to appreciate new ideas brought out by contemporaries.

No one should dismiss the new art forms, because he did not understand them. We were not born with an inherited instinct for the best in art, and our experience showed that it was the thing we understood at first glance that soon became wearisome. The only artist who was sure of his place was the one who contributed some new idea and broke the little conventions of his day. Innovation was one of the qualities that made for lasting success, and because that was so the salvation of art might reasonably come from the amateur instead of the professional artist, who had often to live by repeating himself or other people.

Eveyone was too apt to get out of touch with the aims and ideals of a younger generation, and the stranger and more difficult they appeared the more reason there was to study them. The two ideals that animated the exhibition were the expression of the joyousness of colour and the giving of an emotional synthesis to the artist's feelings.

THE MANCHESTER GUARDIAN,
Friday 24 October 1913

EXPERIMENTS IN ART

Society of Modern Painters' Exhibition

The second annual exhibition of the Society of Modern Painters in Orme's Buildings, Manchester, was opened yesterday by Mr Frank Rutter, the curator of the Leeds Art Gallery.

Mr Charles Hughes, who presided, spoke of the exhibition as interesting and stimulating. It contained, he said, a great deal of excellent work – beautiful design and fine colour and a delightful handling of the material.

Mr Rutter agreed with the Chairman's remark that the exhibition was both interesting and stimulating, and he added that stimulating was not a description which could be given to every art exhibition, because many were dull and depressing. He hoped he would not be misunderstood when he said that one of the great charms of this exhibition was that it contained so little 'clever' work. They were tired of clever work, and what was far more important was sincere work and work which aimed at expressing some emotion the artist had felt. Cleverness was apt to be the bane of modern art. It was so often associated with mediocrity and frequently degenerated to little more than a repetition of what somebody else had done. This exhibition was not merely a repetition or a re-echoing of other people's work. The pictures shown were in the nature of personal experiments, and that was the right attitude for the artist to take up. We had progressed beyond the early Victorian idea that art was merely a question of representation. We asked of a picture not merely that it should tell us what the painter had seen, but what he had thought of what he had seen or felt. The painting must show the mental or emotional state of the artist. Even when the artist was laying rather more stress on the illustrative or decorative side of painting, we asked that he should give us not merely the representation of a landscape but, first of all, his comment upon it. The permanent and increasing interest of a painting depended upon that.

The expression of personality was more clearly understood in music or literature than in painting. It seemed rather extraordinary that the public should pay so much attention to technique in painting – a subject with which they were little acquainted – and should think less of the artist's expression, which was the far more important matter. The artist showed his personality by what he emphasised and what he omitted, and it was only by familiarity with pictures that we were able to discriminate between the best and the second-rate. We could not expect to appreciate all the qualities of a book at the first reading, nor those of a musical composition at the first hearing; and the more there was in a picture the longer it took to appreciate and understand it. It was extraordinarily difficult to appreciate the new ideas of our contemporaries. It was much more easy to appreciate what had gone before us; what other people had explained, and what we were born with a tendency towards. But to appreciate the art of a younger generation was the most difficult thing in the world. We ought not to be in a hurry to dismiss as poor and indifferent or as humbug a new art form which we did not understand. The things we did not understand at the first glance were those which were of real interest to us in the long run.

THE MANCHESTER CITY NEWS,
Saturday 25 October 1913

A MODERN ART SHOW

Can Nature catch up?

For centuries pictorial art has devoted itself to the portrayal of things that can be portrayed, but the pioneers of painting are now pushing gallantly on to portray the things that cannot; the things, so to speak, that aren't there. How they do it is to be seen at the show, now open at the Orme Buildings, Parsonage, of the Society of Modern Painters. It is a big show, in a well-lighted room; it is an interesting show, indeed amazing is not too strong a word. Mr Karl Hagedorn and Mr Malcolm Arbuthnot are the most modern of the moderns whose work assails the eye on these walls, and their visions, not to say nightmares, are a distinct shock at the first blush. Mr Arbuthnot gives harmless names to his creations. He calls them 'The Rhododendrons,' 'The Viaduct', 'Sandhills' and so forth; but Mr Hagedorn has only two titles for all his fifteen or twenty works in watercolour or line etching – 'Rhythmical Expression in Line and Colour,' or 'Rhythmical Expression in Line.' Both men do their very effective best to get away from nature. Mr Arbuthnot's viaduct has two tall arches of red and white bricks, the inside of the arches intensely blue. Through them is seen a little dream-cluster of red-roofed buildings mingled with mill-chimneys, and a vivid streak of green runs along the upper wall of the viaduct. When trees come into his pictures they are of the Noah's Ark type and peacock-gay in solid colour.

Mr Hagedorn's rhythmical expressions include one which happens to be a sea-green man –

Robespierre was pink to him – another seems like a kitchen dresser after an earthquake, a third a badly-broken stained glass window repaired with coloured wools, and a fourth, of which the colour is undeniably harmonious and pleasing, vaguely suggests a rich tesselated pavement violently repressing any tendency to definite pattern. In the etchings the same spirit produces curves and cross-lines such as might haunt the Christmas dream of a school-boy gloomily oppressed with thoughts of Euclid.

It is easy enough to poke fun at these grotesques, but if one candidly seeks their virtues there is to be admitted, in all of them, harmony of colour and a kind of mental excitement in the sinuous or angular antics of the lines – something of the kaleidoscope dazzle, without the kaleidoscope's repetition of design. Sometimes the colour, especially in Mr Arbuthnot's work, strikes you as violent, barbaric. Perhaps he wants it to be like that, and he may take it as a compliment when we say it is just the thing to appeal to very young children. In fact these pioneers suggest Lewis Carrol in paint: as is 'Twas brillig and the slithy toves' to 'Sunset and evening star,' so are these landscapes and buildings and amusing flicks and whirls of colour to 'naturalistic' painting.

Not all the exhibitors are yet in the 'Through the Looking Glass' stage. Some of them produce what we used to understand as pictures, with the gracious 'rhythms' which appealed to less febrile brains. Miss Elizabeth Orme Colles, though now tending to hotter colour, does this kind of work in landscape and portrait – the 'Geoff Nelson' eminent in the latter category. M.S. Nicholls, displaying the recaptured naïveté which is the mark of modernism, has some pleasant, frank studies of Ramsey. Mr E. Rowley-Smart, strongly touched with this same modernism, gets a fine impetuosity into his work, and the bold massive modelling of his mountains, his use of flat colour, and his affected quaintness in portraiture compel attention, often approval. Mr Adolph Valette prefers nature (as seen in Manchester) veiled in mist or fog, and his 'The Irwell' and 'Dover Street' testify to his skill in these essentially Mancestrian scenes. Mr Rowley-Smart's designs for 'King Argimenes' catching well the weirdness of Lord Dunsany's literary imaginings, show him versatile too. Mrs Kate Sargint and Mr Ethel Martin-Frimston are able followers in the art of portraying nature as she must try to be if she is to keep in with modern painting.

Catalogue

All the works listed in the catalogue section are by Karl Hagedorn, unless otherwise indicated. His paintings, watercolours and drawings are listed first in sections one to eight, substantially in chronological order. Then follows his design work, a short section of comparative work by other artists, and finally two miscellaneous items. Since the majority of the works are the property of the Hagedorn Trust, this ownership is assumed unless otherwise indicated.

SECTION ONE

Portraits of the Artist

1　Photographs of the Artist

1 As portrayed on his pass to the *Exposition Universelle* in Brussels, 1910.
2 Probably in Paris, 1912/13. His painting (cat. **15**) is on the table.
3 Around 1930 (?).

2　Self-portrait with Pipe

Oil on canvas laid down on board, 53.5 x 46cms

3　Self-portrait, Painting with Friend

Oil on canvas, 45.5 x 55.5cms

4　Self-portrait

Charcoal and gouache, 38.2 x 25.7cms

5　Self-portrait
Oil on board, 122 x 56cms
Inscribed, bottom right: Karl Hagedorn / 37

6　Caricature of the Artist by Eric Newton

Pencil and gouache, 12.5 x 11.5cms
Inscribed, top right, with EN in monogram (which parodies Hagedorn's monogram)

Newton, who practised as art critic of the *Manchester Guardian* for a time, was a close friend of the artist. Both made designs for *The Unnamed Society* in Manchester. Hagedorn is shown before the kind of industrial background typical of his work around 1920. Newton has employed the characteristically violent colour of Hagedorn's early period, and has also constructed the head using Hagedorn's distinctive arc-based style. Probably made in the early 1920s.

SECTION TWO

Early Works in Manchester and Abroad (1908–12)

The earliest work shown is the book (No. 7) which Hagedorn and his friends compiled in the years 1908 to 1912. It includes a 'family tree' of the group of friends and drawings and watercolours by them. This volume shows Hagedorn developing the use of intense blues which impart a particularly rich mood to the landscapes and buildings which he records.

His views of Paris still show the influence of Adolphe Valette doubtless exerted through Valette's rôle as a teacher in Manchester.

Gradually a more modern approach surfaces in figures portrayed with rhythmic contours, perhaps under the influence of Matisse, although Hagedorn's Parisian master, Maurice Denis, must also have had an effect.

7　Der Künstler Zwei

Loose-leaf volume containing drawings by members of the *Der Künstler Zwei* group of which Hagedorn was a founder member. The drawings are mainly by Hagedorn and Francis Sladen Smith who travelled with him in 1912 and 13, and who exhibited with him in Paris. Hagedorn visited Freiburg, Feltre (in the Tyrol) and Beni Mora.

8　Leaf from a Scrapbook : Harry Coller at the Piano

Pencil and ink on an envelope, 25.5 x 11.5cms
Inscribed, left: 'Arry' ; right: KAJ Hagedorn; bottom left: the monogram of the *Der Künstler Zwei* group

The postmark on the envelope records that it was posted in Liverpool WC1 at 8.10pm on November 16th 1911. Judging from the coloured paper on which the envelope is mounted, and from the monogram, the drawing originally formed part of the journal of the *Der Künstler Zwei* group.

9 Old Trafford Swing Bridge

Etching, 20 x 13.5cms
Probably made in 1911.

10 Iron Bridge on the Irwell

Etching, 18 x 12.8cms

This print, and cat. **9**, display the influence of
Adolphe Valette who taught at the Manchester
School of Art when Hagedorn attended it
Probably done in 1911

11 Domed Church in a Landscape

Pencil and watercolour, 29 x 22.5cms
Inscribed, bottom right, with the artist's monogram

12 Domed Church in a Landscape

Etching, 12.5 x 7.5cms
Inscribed, in the margin bottom right : Karl
Hagedorn / 1912

Probably developed from the site studied in the
comparable watercolour (cat. 11)

13 Paris, Bridges on the Seine

Pencil and watercolour, 22.2 x 30.2cms
Inscribed, bottom right : K. Hagedorn 1912

The drawing is laid down on the dark brown paper
employed for the journal of the *Der Künstler Zwei*
group.

14 Canal Boat moored by a Factory

Pencil and watercolour, 24 x 32cms
Inscribed, bottom right, with the monogram and
date 12

Despite the resemblance of the scene to a typical
Manchester location, it may well have been studied
in Paris.

15 Paris : St. Sulpice

Oil on board, 39.5 x 32cms
Inscribed: on label on reverse : Karl Hagedorn /
Manchester / St. Sulpice Paris 1912 / £1-1-0

16 On the Beach

Pencil and watercolour, 20 x 25cms
Inscribed, top right : K. HAGEDORN.12
Exhibited at the Salon d'Automne, Paris 1912

Lent by the Ivy Restaurant, London

17 Figure playing a Lyre in a Landscape

Pencil, watercolour and gouache, 20 x 25cms

18 Woman in a Landscape

Pencil and watercolour, 26 x 22cms
The paper has a French watermark

19 Female Figure in a Doorway

Pencil and watercolour, 26.7 x 20cms
On the reverse : similar composition in pencil

43 (cat. 13)

20 Two Compositions with Female Nudes

Pen and ink, and gouache, 16.8 x 27cms
On the reverse, the left-hand composition in
reversed colours.

21 Two Compositions : Each with a Female
Nude in an Interior

Linocut in brown ink, 13.2 x 11cms each

22 Walking Nude

Gouache, 42 x 26.5cms

Lent by the Ivy Restaurant, London

23 Woman in Regional Costume

Gouache, 48 x 32cms
The paper has a French watermark

SECTION THREE

Nude Studies (1912–13)

At this time, Hagedorn began to study the figure by
employing facets or cubes, clearly under the influence
of Cubist paintings and, perhaps more important,
sculpture which he would have seen in Paris.

24 Kneeling Nude

Watercolour, 28.5 x 20.5cms
Inscribed, bottom right, with the monogram and
date 13

Private collection

25 Standing Nude

Watercolour, 33 x 23cms
Inscribed, top right: Feb 22nd 1913

Private Collection

26 Reclining Nude

Watercolour, 25 x 32.5cms
Inscribed, bottom right: May 23rd

Undoubtedly painted on May 23rd 1913

27 Nude on One Knee

Watercolour, 24.7 x 23cms

Private Collection

28 Reclining Nude

Pencil and watercolour, 22.8 x 30.3cms

Probably painted in early 1913

29 Two Female Nudes

Pencil, 31.2 x 24.1cms
On the reverse : Female Nude
Inscribed, on the reverse bottom right : October
Probably drawn in 1912

30 Standing Nude

Pencil, 32 x 21.5cms

31 Standing Nude from Behind

Pencil, 32.5 x 22cms

32 Reclining Nude

Pencil, 24 x 32.3cms

33 Reclining Nude

Pencil, 25 x 32cms

34 Kneeling Female Nude 'Primitive' Style

Pen and ink with brush, 38.2 x 25.7cms

35 Female Nude

Ink and brush, 32.5 x 25cms
Inscribed, bottom right, in brush: Karl Hagedorn

44 (cat. **36**)

36 Female Nude

Pen and ink, 38 x 25.7cms

SECTION FOUR

*Manchester's First Modernist: the 1913
Exhibition and its Aftermath (1913–1916)*

Hagedorn's period as an avowed modernist lasted
from 1913 when the majority of his advanced works
were made until Spring 1916 when he went to war.
Hagedorn declared that he had set out to bring the
new form of art to Manchester and described his
work of that period as 'Expressionist'.

Some of the works in this section are definitely
identifiable as having been shown in the 1913 Exhibition; others we assume were there. Cat. **43–47**
may well be slightly later, but may well have been
thought of as 'Rhythmical Expressions'.

The works of this period show a welter of influences from cubism and futurism, and from the
Omega Workshops.

37 Rhythmical Expression : Washstand

Oil on canvas, laid down on board, 52 x 44.5cms

This painting, exhibited in the 1913 Exhibition of
the Society of Modern Painters, Manchester, was
illustrated in the outraged article in the *Daily Mail*
of 23rd October that year. See the essay by Alistair
Smith above.

The Whitworth Art Gallery

38 Rhythmical Expression : Fishing Boats

Oil on canvas, laid down on board, 44.5 x 53cms

Exhibited at the 1913 Exhibition of the Society
of Modern Painters, Manchester.

**39 Rhythmical Expression : Portrait of a
Woman**

Oil on canvas, laid on board, 53.5 x 46cms
Inscribed, top right, with the monogram and date 13

**40 Rhythmical Expression : Landscape with
Tower**

Oil on canvas, 53.5 x 45.5cms
Inscribed with the monogram and date 13

41 Rhythmical Expression : Abstract

Pen and ink and gouache, 26 x 21cms

42 Rhythmical Expression : Washstand?

Pencil and watercolour, 34.5 x 27cms

Perhaps a study for the oil painting cat. **37**.

**43 Rhythmical Expression : Two Figures in a
Landscape**

Pencil, pen and ink, 27.4 x 19.7cms

44 Rhythmical Expression : Teapot

Pencil and black ink on paper, 24.2 x 21.2cms

45 Rhythmical Expression : Landscape with Figures

Black ink on paper, 26 x 21.2cms

46 Rhythmical Expression : Bathers

Pencil and black ink on paper, 23.4 x 19.2cms

47 Bathers

Oil on canvas, 91.5 x 46.5cms

For contemporary critical assessment of his painting, see Alistair Smith's essay (p. 19).

Lent by the Ivy Restaurant, London

48 Village Street

Oil on canvas laid down on board, 54.5 x 45.5cms
Inscribed, bottom left: Karl Hagedorn/16

49 Design for Poster : Society of Modern Artists

Pen and ink, and gouache on paper, 76 x 52cms
Inscribed, top right: Karl Hagedorn / 16
Lettering: EXHIBITION / Society of Modern / MODERN.PAINTER/S

Hagedorn employed one of the African sculptures which he had probably acquired in Paris, for this autograph poster, advertising the exhibition of March 1916.

Lent by the Coughton Galleries Ltd, Arthingworth

SECTION FIVE

Wartime

Hagedorn became a British subject in 1914, and married in 1915. He is known to have been a Lance-corporal in the Middlesex regiment, and his war lasted from 1916 to Spring 1919. His landscape studies showed that he was close to areas where heavy fighting took place. Some of them were exhibited after his return to this country.

50 A Camp in Flanders

Pencil and watercolour on paper, 20.5 x 26.5cms (sight)
Inscribed, top right, with the monogram and date 17
A label on the reverse is inscribed: A CAMP IN FLANDERS / £5-5-0 (erased) / KARL HAGEDORN / 24 ROWAN AVENUE / MANCHESTER

51 Sand Quarry

Pencil and watercolour, 22.5 x 32.2cms (sight)
Inscribed, top left, with the monogram and date 17
On the reverse a label: A SAND QUARRY / £5-5-0 KARL HAGEDORN / 24 ROWAN AVENUE / MANCHESTER

52 Reclining Soldier, Reading

Pen and ink, 20.5 x 33.5cms

53 Reclining Soldier, Reading

Pen and ink, 20.5 x 33.5cms

54 Man at Rest

Pen and ink, 33 x 20.3cms

55 Seated Man
Pen and ink, 35.5 x 20.5cms

56 Portrait of a Young Man in Uniform

Pencil, 35.5 x 25cms
Inscribed, top right: May 24th 18 / 'Miky'

57 Landscape : Cassel

Watercolour, 24 x 34.5cms (sight)
Inscribed, top right, with the artist's monogram and the date 18. On the reverse (in modern hand): 'Cassel' from South

Cassel was the headquarters of the Second British Army, 1916–18. It had a commanding view of the battlefield near Ypres.

Lent by the Coughton Galleries Ltd., Arthingworth

58 Landscape : Mount Kemmel

Pen and ink, and watercolour on paper, 25 x 35cms (sight)
Inscribed, top right, with the artist's monogram and the date 19

45 (cat. **56**)

Label on reverse (in modern hand) : 307 Mount Lemmel from Wyshart, 28th March

The label, despite its inaccuracies, surely transcribes an inscription hidden by the mount. The location is Mount Kemmel seen from Wytschaete, an area which saw heavy fighting and changes of possession throughout the war. Hagedorn was there on 28th March 1919 to record the scene. This may be the *Devastated Area, Mount Kemmel* which he exhibited in July 1919 at the Allied Artists' Association.

Lent by the Coughton Galleries Ltd , Arthingworth

59 Poster : The Dover Patrol Fund

Pencil and gouache, 65.5 x 43cms
Lettering: The Dover Patrol Fund / Roll up and See / 'So am I' / at the / New Theatre Hazebrouck / Rue de Clocher / All proceeds to the Above Fund / 18 hours / Feb.23.24.25.1919

SECTION SIX

After the War: Landscape (1919–1923)

It was in these years that Hagedorn developed his distinctive style of geometric landscape. First, he studied the industrial townscape, principally in Stockport. After his removal to Buxton in 1922, Derbyshire began to feature and the works of 1922 and 1923 saw the peak of his landscape work in this style.

60 Babbacombe Bay

Pencil and watercolour, 24.5 x 34.2cms
Inscribed, top right, with the monogram and date 19

Babbacombe Bay is a popular beach near Torquay. The Hagedorns obviously celebrated the end of the war there.

46 (cat. **61**)

61 Quarry workers

Pencil and watercolour, 34 x 50.4cms
Inscribed, top right, with the monogram and date 20

62 Dockland Panorama

Pencil and watercolour, 24 x 35.2cms
Inscribed, bottom right, with the monogram and date 20

Probably a location studied in the Manchester area.

63 Stockport

Pen and ink, and watercolour, 34 x 50cms
Inscribed, top left, with the monogram and date 20
On the reverse, a card with the inscription: Karl Hagedorn, 24 Rowan Avenue, Whalley Range, Manchester / STOCKPORT VIADUCT, WATERCOLOUR, £10.10s. Painted June 1920

The building in the foreground is identified as the 'Stokport Hippodrome'.

Lent by J.G. Dean Esq.

64 Stockport

Pencil, pen and ink, and watercolour, 35 x 51.5cms
Inscribed, top right, with the monogram and date 20

65 Macclesfield

Pencil, pen and ink, and watercolour, 34.5 x 51.5cms
Inscribed, top right with the monogram and date 20

66 The School Yard

Pen and ink, and watercolour, 26.4 x 20cms
Inscribed, top right: K. Hagedorn 21
On a label on the reverse (in modern hand): (Marked on Back) / 'The School Yard' / From the Studio at Blakely and Beving about 1921, Karl Hagedorn

The Beving family had business connections with Germany and it was perhaps because of this that Hagedorn found himself in their Stockport office. The label on the reverse obviously records an inscription hidden by the mount.

Lent by L.J. Olivier Esq.

67 Portrait of a Young Man

Pencil and watercolour, 53 x 36cms
Inscribed, top right, with the monogram, and date 22

68 Two Viaducts

Pen and ink, and watercolour, 74 x 55cms
Inscribed, bottom right: Karl Hagedorn / 22

Lent by Mrs. S. Olivier

69 Woman and Dog in a Landscape with Viaduct

Pen and ink, and watercolour, 74 x 55cms
Inscribed, bottom right: Karl Hagedorn / 22

Lent by Mrs. S. Olivier

70 Burford

Pencil and watercolour, 33.5 x 50cms
Inscribed, top left, with the artist's monogram and
date 23
On the reverse: Burford 1922/23

Probably studied at Burford in Shropshire.

71 Buxton

Pen and ink, and watercolour, 34.5 x 50.5cms
Inscribed, top right: Karl Hagedorn 23 and beneath
the mount: Buxton

72 Buxton from Westbourne

Pencil, pen and ink, and watercolour, 36.5 x 52 cms
Inscribed, bottom centre, beneath the mount:
Buxton from Westbourne

The artist studied the scene from his studio window. He lived near Buxton from 1922 to 1927 and
played an active part in the affairs of the local art
society.

73 Topley Pike

Pencil, pen and ink, and watercolour, 36 x 52cms
Inscribed, top right: K Hagedorn 23; and, beneath
the mount: Topley Pike.

Topley Pike is in Derbyshire

74 Chesterfield

Pencil, pen and ink, and watercolour, 44 x 35cms
Inscribed, bottom left: Karl Hagedorn 23

75 Farmyard with Chickens

Pen and ink, and watercolour on paper, 35 x 51cms
Inscribed, top right: Karl Hagedorn 1923
On the reverse (in modern hand): Shire Oaks /
Derbyshire 1919-25, probably transcribing an
inscription hidden by the mount.

Lent by the Coughton Galleries Ltd , Arthingworth

76 Farm in France

Pen and ink, and watercolour, 35 x 51cms
Inscribed, top right, with the monogram and date 23

Lent by L.J. Olivier Esq.

SECTION SEVEN

Travel (1925)

This series of watercolours was made during holidays spent in Italy and the French Riviera, when
Hagedorn developed a quicker, broader technique,
and showed a greater interest in representing what
he saw, rather than producing a geometrical pattern.

77 Continental Harbour Scene

Pencil and watercolour, 33.5 x 50cms
Inscribed, bottom right, with the monogram and
date 25

78 Harbour Scene

Pencil and watercolour, 49.5 x 33cms
Inscribed, top left: K. Hagedorn 25

79 Continental Church with Market Stalls in Foreground

Pencil and watercolour, 50 x 33.5cms
Inscribed, bottom left, beneath the mount:
Hagedorn 25

80 Piazza with Church and People

Pencil and watercolour, 33.5 x 50cms
Inscribed, top left, with the monogram and date 25

81 Continental Village with Church

Pencil and watercolour, 36.5 x 55cms
Inscribed, top left, with the monogram and date 25

82 San Remo

Pencil and watercolour, 49 x 33cms
Inscribed, top left: Hagedorn 25; bottom right,
beneath the mount: San Remo 1925.

47 (cat. **82**)

83 Col de Rodi

Pencil and watercolour, 35 x 50.5cms
Inscribed, bottom right: Colderodi; and beneath
the mount: 1925

The village is close to St. Tropez on the French
Riviera. It is so called because the original settle-
ment was founded by a group of the Knights of
Rhodes when shipwrecked there in the twelfth
century.

84 Continental Village Scene with Church and Tower

Pencil and watercolour, 33.4 x 50cms
Inscribed, top right, with the monogram and date 26

85 Mountain Village with Bridge

Pencil and watercolour, 31.6 x 49cms

SECTION EIGHT

1926 Onwards

A selection of works chronicling the style employed by Hagedorn during the remainder of his working life. He appeared to have mixed views about his later style, sometimes regretting the abandonment of his modernist work. See the essay by Leslie Worth above.

86 'Aunt Nelly in Avignon'

Pencil and watercolour, 40 x 57cms
Inscribed, bottom left: Avignon 1926

87 St. Tropez

Pencil, and black crayon, 34.5 x 40.8cms
Inscribed, bottom right: 1928 of St. Tropez / Cartoon for Calendar and paint

One of the boats is named *Trois Amis / Toulon* (see cat. **88**).

88 Sailing Boats

Pencil and watercolour on paper, 50.5 x 32.5cms
Inscribed on the right-hand boat: TROIS AMIS

Private Collection

89 St. Tropez

Pencil, pen and ink, and gouache, 33 x 51cms
Inscribed, bottom left: St. Tropez 1928 Karl Hagedorn

Private Collection

90 Sailing-boat, 'The Discovery'

Pencil and watercolour, 50.4 x 31.4cms
Inscribed, label on reverse: 'The Discovery' / Karl Hagedorn / 35gms / 12

91 Large Tree with Woman in Foreground

Pencil and watercolour, 52 x 34cms
Inscribed, bottom right, with the monogram and date 29

92 The Artist's Wife and Friends on Holiday

Pen and ink, and brush on paper, 31.5 x 43.2cms
Inscribed: The Schwabes, Singer & Johnny & Nell at Lanligos (?) 1932

Randolph Schwabe, born in Manchester, was four years older than Hagedorn. He was Professor at the Slade School of Art, from 1930 until his death in 1948, and exerted a decisive influence on Hagedorn's work. See the essay by Leslie Worth above.

93 'The Chambers Boys at Marlow'

Pen and ink, and wash on paper, 30.1 x 41cms

94 Beach Scene : Hastings

Pen and ink, and watercolour on paper, 34.8 x 50cms
Inscribed: Kicking Jack / Hastings / Karl Hagedorn 1933

Hagedorn exhibited this delightful view at his one-man exhibition at the Fine Art Society, London, in 1934.

95 The Large Tree at Kilton

Pen and ink, and watercolour, 34.5 x 52cms
Inscribed, bottom left, beneath the mount: Kilton 1933

96 Farmyard

Black crayon, pencil, and watercolour, 35.5 x 51cms
Inscribed, bottom right: Citre (?) 1933

97 The Cathedral Square, Freiburg-im-Breisgau

Pen and ink, and watercolour on paper,
33.5 x 45cms
Inscribed, bottom right: Karl Hagedorn 1935 /
Freiburg i/B

Educated in Freiburg-im-Breisgau, which is situated
between Strasbourg and Basle, Hagedorn visited his
aunts there every year.

Lent by the Coughton Galleries Ltd., Arthingworth

98 Portuguese Fishermen

Pen and ink, and watercolour, 28 x 44cms
Inscribed, bottom right: Karl Hagedorn 36
On the reverse, a label was inscribed:
Karl Hagedorn RBA / 59b Belsize Park Gardens NW3
Portuguese Fishermen

Exhibited at the Exhibition of the Society of
Modern Painters held at the Whitworth Art
Gallery in 1937.

The Whitworth Art Gallery

99 Roadworkers Digging Trench

Oil on plywood, 76 x 63.5cms
Inscribed, bottom right: Karl Hagedorn / 38

100 Avignon, from Villeneuve

Watercolour, 33.7 x 46.2cms
Inscribed, bottom left: Karl Hagedorn 39

The view is across the River Rhone and shows the
Papal Palace in the distance.

The Whitworth Art Gallery

101 Still-life : Chickens and Feltham Church

Gouache on paper, 44 x 52.5cms
Inscribed, bottom right: Karl Hagedorn 42

102 Still-life with Horse-chestnut

Ink and watercolour on paper, 65.8 x 49.5cms
Inscribed illegibly, bottom right, under the mount,
but dated 1947

103 Radio Masts near Rugby

Pen and ink, and watercolour, 34.7 x 50cms
The drawing is made on the reverse of a map of
Canada

104 Harbour Scene (Malta?)

Pencil and watercolour, 30 x 44.5cms (to the border)
Inscribed, top left: from our window at the . . . .;
top right: Sunday. Also some mounting instructions
beneath the mount

105 Three Bridges from Cannon Street

Pen and ink, and watercolour , 41.6 x 29.5cms
Inscribed, bottom right: Karl Hagedorn 60; left,
beneath the mount: New Wash Mount; right,
beneath the mount: Sept. 13th 1960, 3 bridges from
Canon Street No. 5

50 (cat. **99**)

106 Little Boltons

Crayon, ink and watercolour, 35 x 24cms
Inscribed, top left: 10 Nov. 1963. (33)

SECTION NINE

Design

Hagedorn's training as a textile designer at the Municipal School of Technology at Manchester spanned
the time from October 1906 to November 1907 at
least. His practice of textile design is, unfortunately,
impossible to exemplify significantly in the exhibition, but his talent for design lies at the basis of most
of his paintings and drawings, and surfaced more
overtly in designs for advertising. He worked for the
Radio Times and, later in life, for Shell. His Shippers'
Tickets (cat. **134, 135, 136**) won him an award at
the Decorative Arts Exhibition in Paris in 1925.

107 Poster: Society of Modern Painters Exhibition

Pen and ink, and gouache, 76 x 52cms
Inscribed, top right: Karl Hagedorn / 16
Lettering: EXHIBITION / Society of Modern /
MODERN PAINTER / S

The African sculpture belonged to the artist (cat.
163). The exhibition took place in May 1916.
Hagedorn exhibited twelve items in the *Etchings
and Watercolours* section, and seven oil paintings.
Notable amongst these was his *Bathers* painting
(ill. 24). It had already been praised in the press,
which probably partially accounted for the high
price asked (£36.15.0). The artist may also have
been reluctant to sell. Hagedorn also showed one
Rhythmical Arrangement in Colour and Line; *The Quay
(a Rhythmical Study)* and a watercolour of *Granville*

which he had used to illustrate his article on Expressionism in the *Manchester Playgoer* of July 1914.

Lent by the Coughton Galleries Ltd, Arthingworth

108 Poster : Society of Modern Painters Exhibition

Print, 73 x 48.3cms
Signed, top right: Hagedorn
On the reverse, a label: RA / Karl Hagedorn / Window Bill / Exhibition of Art in Industry April 20th to May 4th
Lettering: SOCIETY OF MODERN PAINTERS / EXHIBITION / 2 MOUNT STREET, ALBERT SQUARE, MANCHESTER

For the 1926 Exhibition.

109 Design for a Poster : St. Paul's Cathedral

Pen and ink, and watercolour, 57.5 x 41cms (sight)
Titled at the top and signed, bottom right: Karl Hagedorn excud 1923.

This design was never printed. Hagedorn probably used the design, and its companions (cat. 110,111) to try to obtain a commission from the Underground Electric Railways Co. of London Ltd., or from the London Public Transport Board.

Private Collection

110 Design for a Poster : Trafalgar Square and the National Gallery

Pen and ink, and watercolour, 57 x 41cms (sight)
Titled at the top and signed, bottom right: Karl Hagedorn excud 1924

Private Collection

111 Design for a Poster : The Tower of London

Pen and ink, and watercolour, 57 x 41cms (sight)
Titled at the top and signed, bottom right: Karl Hagedorn excud 1924

Private Collection

112 Poster : Buy British

Print, 77 x 51cms
Signed, lower left: KH
Lettering: BUY BRITISH / SWB 11 ISSUED BY THE EMPIRE MARKETING BOARD / PRINTED FOR HM STATIONERY OFFICE BY MALBY & SONS / 1027.P.1662.230.EST NO.4360.20.000.11.27.

The original design for this poster is in the Victoria and Albert Museum (no. E 328-1934), to whom it was donated by the Empire Marketing Board. R.D. Gossop, whose name is written on the reverse of the poster, illustrated it in his article *How buyers of design have reacted to 'modern art' during the past twenty five years.* (Penrose Annual, Vol 37, 1935, p. 17).

See Stephen Constantine, *Buy and Build : The Advertising Posters of the Empire Marketing Board*, London 1986.

113 Design for Poster : Underground

Pencil, pen and ink, and gouache, 75 x 50.5cms
Signed: HAGEDORN
Lettering: TO THE THEATRES BY / UNDER-GROUND

This design, and cat. 114–124 seem never to have been printed. They probably served as a portfolio to exemplify Hagedorn's work.

114 Design for Poster : GWR

Pencil and gouache, 41 x 28cms
Signed, top right: HAGEDORN
Lettering: INTO THE SUNSHINE / BY / G.W.R.

115 Design for Poster : The Sunny Countryside

Pencil and gouache, 75 x 50cms
Signed, on left: KARL HAGEDORN
Lettering: THE / SUNNY / COUNTRYSIDE

116 Design for Poster : Batik

Pencil and gouache, 75 x 51.5cms
Signed, top left: HAGEDORN
Lettering: TUTANKHAMUN COMES BACK TO LIFE / A STORY TOLD IN BATIK

117 Design for a Poster : The Pipe of Peace

Pencil and gouache, 73.7 x 53cms
Signed, top right: KARL HAGEDORN
Lettering: THE PIPE OF PEACE

118 Design for Poster : Margarine

Pencil and gouache, 75.5 x 50.5cms
Signed, on right: KARL HAGEDORN
Lettering: MARGARINE / DON'T FORGET IT MUM

119 Design for Poster : Electric Lamps

Pencil and gouache, 75 x 49.5cms
Signed: KARL HAGEDORN
Lettering: ELECTRIC LAMPS / OF INCOMPAR-ABLE POWER

120 Design for Poster : Washing Powder

Pencil and gouache, 78 x 53cms
Signed: KARL HAGEDORN
Lettering: WASHING POWDER / MAKES WASH-ING CHILD'S PLAY

121 Design for Poster : Toothpaste

Pencil and gouache, 76.5 x 49.5cms
Signed, on right: KARL HAGEDORN
Lettering (on the tube): TOOTHPASTE and TOOTHPASTE / WORTH UNTO GOLD

122 Design : The Laboratory

Pencil and gouache, 28 x 20.5cms
Signed, bottom centre: KH

123 Design : The Engine

Pencil and gouache, 28 x 20.5cms
Signed, bottom centre: KH
The paper has a French watermark and is marked with holes from compasses

124 Design : Weaving

Pen and ink, and gouache, 28 x 20.5cms
Signed, bottom centre: KH

Lent by the Coughton Galleries Ltd, Arthingworth

125 Design : Never Fade Fabrics

Print, 48 x 38.5cms
Signed, top right: HAGEDORN
Lettering: A STANDARD OF QUALITY / Solprufe regd / FABRICS / GUARANTEED FAST TO SUN-LIGHT AND WASHING / PRINTED BY JOHN ALBINSON LTD., OLDHAM

126 Design : Hill Town with Cypresses

Gouache, 28.2 x 25.5cms
On the reverse, a label: T. Haynes, Chorley, Colour Printers

127 Design : A Wise Bird Knows

Pencil, pen and ink, and watercolour, 33.5 x 23cms
Signed, on left: HAGEDORN
Lettering: A WISE BIRD KNOWS
On the reverse, a label inscribed: Hagedorn, and R.P. Gossop, Artists' Agent, Henrietta Street, WC2. Gossop was known for his articles on design (see cat. 112)

128 Design : Daffodils

Pencil and gouache, 29 x 20.5cms
On the reverse, a label identifies the design as being the property of Horrocks & Co. Ltd., Town Hall Works, Ashton-under-Lyne

129 Design : Advertisement for Horrocks Shirtings

Pen and ink, and gouache, 24.5 x 15cms
Signed, top left: Hagedorn; at bottom: Horrocks Shirtings

130 Poster : Osman Towels

Print, 33 x 21.5cms
Lettering: Osman / TOWELS
Signed, top left: Hagedorn

This design was developed from the original *Bathers* composition of 1913/15. See cat. **46** and **47**.

Lent by L.J. Olivier, Esq.

131 Design : Advertisement for Osman Sheets

Pen and ink, and gouache, 34.5 x 23.1cms
Signed, top left: Hagedorn
Lettering: OSMAN / SHEETS / FOR STRENGTH / AND ENDURANCE

On the reverse, the label of R.D. Gossop, Artist's Agent (see cat. 112)

132 Design : Textile Mill

Pen and ink, watercolour and gouache, 17.5 x 20cms
Signed, bottom left: Hagedorn

Lent by the Coughton Galleries Ltd, Arthingworth

133 Design : Radio Times Cover, Summer 1929

Print, 32 x 29.5 cms
Signed, bottom right: Hagedorn
Lettering: RADIO TIMES / 3d / SUMMER NUMBER; and in the top margin: Radio Times, August 2, 1929. Vol. 24. No. 305 [Registered at the GPO as a newspaper]. North of England Edition.

134 Shippers' Tickets

Print, 14 x 9cms each
1 La Bolsa
2 La Catedral
3 Nodescolora
4 Plaza del Mercado
5 El Monumento
6 La Yunta
Shippers' tickets were used to identify cotton goods during transport. These won Hagedorn his Grand Prix at the Exposition Internationale des Arts Decoratifs et Industriels of 1925 in Paris. NH Dick in *Shippers' Tickets* (Penrose Annual, Vol XXIX, 1927, p44) described them as 'treated in the modern manner, and yet in a way that is acceptable to the most conservative. These tickets show how essentially suitable modern conventions in painting may be for commercial uses....'

135 Shippers' Tickets

Print, 14 x 9cms each
1 Salida del Sol
2 Hijo de Sevilla
3 El Panadero
4 Sangre Torero
5 Los Aficionados

136 Shippers' Tickets

Print, 14 x 9cms each
1 El pavo
2 Los Jugadores
3 La Siesta
4 Hija de Madrid
5 Los Dos Gatos
6 El Ramo de Cambur

137 Design for Book Cover : The Smokeless City

Pencil, pen and ink, and gouache, 22 x 14cms
Signed, top left, K. Hagedorn 22
Lettering: THE SMOKELESS CITY / BY E.D. SIMON & MARION FITZGERALD

In the event, the design was not used although the

book was published. E.D. Simon (Baron Simon of Wythenshawe) and his co-author put the view that it was domestic fires which were principally responsible for smoke-filled cities like Manchester.

138 Design : Carousel

Pen and ink on paper, 22.5 x 22.5cms
Signed, bottom left: HAGEDORN
On the reverse (in modern hand): 'Oldham Panto-mime'

Lent by the Coughton Galleries Ltd, Arthingworth

139 Design : The Hospital Book

Print, 39 x 25cms
Signed, bottom left of the design: Hagedorn
Lettering: HOSPITAL BOOK / MANCHESTER AND SALFORD / MEDICAL CHARITIES 1925

Hagedorn was involved in the design of this book whose sale raised money for hospital charities.

Private Collection

140 Design for Theatrical Costumes

Pencil and watercolour, 18 x 23cms
Signed bottom left: K. Hagedorn

This watercolour records the costumes designed by Hagedorn for *The Unnamed Society*, a Manchester group which wrote and produced avant-garde plays with modernist settings and costumes. The costumes were for the play *Harbour* by L. Stanley Jast, which formed part of a triple bill performance on 18th October 1921. It was subsequently performed at the Margaret Morris Theatre, Flood Street, Chelsea. The characters, from left to right, are The Chorus, The Image of the Buddha and The Pilgrim.
See: *The Unnamed Book*, Manchester 1924

SECTION TEN

Designs for the Manchester University Rag

Hagedorn volunteered his services for the University Rag for the first time in 1924, when he was developing a portfolio of designs (Nos. 107-111), perhaps in an effort to gain commissions. He worked on the Rag for a time even after his removal to London in 1927.

141 The Rag Rag

Print, each 24 x 18.5cms
1 The Rag Rag 1926 (Chimpanzee and Serpent)
2 The Rag Rag 1927 (Dancers with Sun and Serpent)
3 The Rag Rag 1928 (Serpent as Jack-in-the Box)

Three editions of the publication of the Manchester University Annual Rag. Hagedorn designed posters and also book covers for the Rag from 1924 to 1934, not being involved in the years 1931 to 33. His designs usually incorporate the sun and/or serpent from the University coat-of-arms.

The Whitworth Art Gallery

142 Poster: Manchester Rag Rag 1927

Print, 76 x 50.5cms
Signed, bottom right: Hagedorn
Lettering: The / Rag Rag / Unviersity of Manchester / Shrove Tuesday 1927 / 'Streuth in Advertising / Musical Supplement with every copy / Horrock & Co. Ltd. / Printers / Ashton-under-Lyne

143 Design for Cover of The Rag Rag 1928

Print with gouache emendations, 53.5 x 41.5cms
Signed, top left: Hagedorn

144 Design for Poster: University of Manchester Annual Rag Magazine 1929

Print with gouache emendations, 55.4 x 41.6cms
The signature, Hagedorn, is incorporated into the design at bottom left

145 Poster: The Rag Rag 1934

Print, 77 x 51cms
Titled at top, and lettered at bottom: UNIVERSI-TY OF MANCHESTER / RAG ANNUAL and BETTER THAN NEVER! and dated 1934
Bottom left: C. Nicholls & Co. Ltd. / The Philips Park Press

Private Collection

146 Printed Design: The Rag Rag 1934

Print, 24 x 18.5cms
Signed: Hagedorn
Lettering: THE RAG RAG / 1934 / UNIVERSITY OF MANCHESTER / RAG ANNUAL

This design was used as the cover of the Rag publication in 1934

147 Design: University of Manchester Rag Rag 1930

Print with gouache emendations, 55.5 x 41.8cms
Signed, centre right: Hagedorn

SECTION ELEVEN

Works by Other Artists

Vanessa Bell (1879–1961)
148 Triple Alliance (Still Life)

Collage with paper, oil paint and pastel, 81.9 x 60.3cms
Made about 1914

Lent by the University of Leeds Art Collections

Vanessa Bell (1879–1961)
149 White IV

Printed linen, 80.5 x 51cms
Stamped with the symbol of the Omega Workshops for which Bell made the design in 1913. Printed in France.

The Whitworth Art Gallery

David Bomberg (1890–1957)
150 Study for 'Sappers at Work. A Canadian Tunnelling Company'

Conté crayon, 27.9 x 40.6cms
Made about 1918

The Whitworth Art Gallery

Roger Fry (1866–1934)
151 Chauvigny

Oil on canvas, 61 x 91.4cms
Inscribed, bottom left: Roger Fry 1911

Lent by the University of Leeds Art Collection

Roger Fry (1886–1934)
152 Amenophis III

Printed linen, 46 x 80cms

Designed in 1913 for the Omega Workshops and printed in France. The design was derived from an oil painting by Fry, showing a *Still-life: Eggs and Books.* The jug shape is very similar to that in Hagedorn's *Rhythmical Expression: Washstand* (cat. **37**).

The Whitworth Art Gallery

Henri Gaudier-Brzeska (1891–1915)
153 The Family

Pen and ink, 38.5 x 25.3cms
Inscribed, bottom left, with the artist's monogram

The Whitworth Art Gallery

Duncan Grant (1885–1978)
154 Abstract Design

Pencil and gouache, 60.9 x 48cms

Made by Grant as part of his work for The Omega Workshops, about 1914.

Lent by the Courtauld Institute Galleries (Gift: Pamela Diamond 1958)

Percy Wyndham Lewis (1882–1957)
155 Girl Asleep

Pen and ink, and watercolour, 28 x 58.5cms
Inscribed, bottom right: Wyndham Lewis. 1911

Lent by Manchester City Art Galleries

Percy Wyndham Lewis (1882–1957)
156 The Lascar

Pen and ink, and watercolour, 30.5 x 28cms
Inscribed, bottom left: W.L. 1919

The Whitworth Art Gallery

C.R.W. Nevinson (1889–1946)
157 On Brooklyn Bridge

Drypoint, 23.5 x 17.2cms
Inscribed: C.R.W. Nevinson; and (by another hand), on Brooklyn Bridge

The Whitworth Art Gallery

William Roberts (1895–1980)
The Boxing Match, Novices

Pencil and watercolour, 50.9 x 35.6cms
Inscribed, bottom left: William Roberts

The Whitworth Art Gallery

Adolphe Valette (1876–1942)
159 The Irwell, Manchester

Oil on canvas, 143.5 x 86.3cms
Painted in 1913

Lent by Mr and Mrs Martin Green

Edward Wadsworth (1889–1949)
160 Granite Quarries, Darby Hill, Oldbury, Worcs.

Pen and indian ink, 25.3 x 36.7cms (sight)
Inscribed, bottom left: Edward Wadsworth. 1919

The Whitworth Art Gallery

Edward Wadsworth (1889–1949)
161 The Open Window

Colour woodcut, 16.2 x 11.1cms
Inscribed: The Open Window
Made around 1914

The Whitworth Art Gallery

Edward Wadsworth (1889–1949)
162 Dazzle Camouflage: Ship in Dry Dock

Woodcut, 12.5 x 21.5cms
Made in 1918

The Whitworth Art Gallery

SECTION TWELVE
Miscellaneous

163 African Sculpture

Painted wood, with additional beads, height 37cms

This sculpture was certainly in Hagedorn's possession by the time of the 1913 exhibition of the Society of Modern Painters. It featured in one of his paintings in the exhibition, as documented by the photograph of the party on the closing night. Hagedorn also included it in a painting of 1915 (now lost, but see ill. 4) and in his poster of the Society's 1916 exhibition (cat. **107**).

164 Cigarette

Cigarette, mounted on Hagedorn's visiting card, with hand-made envelope. Inscribed, on the visiting card: "24 JUNI 1912" CIGARETTE VON MATISSE IN SEINEM ATELIER mit ihm GERAUCHT and on the envelope: Juni 24.1912, Besuch bei Matisse, 92 Rue de Clamart, mit Rik von Hool

The inscriptions record the smoking of the cigarette in Matisse's studio, which Hagedorn visited in June 1912 with Rik von Hool.

Private Collection